Building Sunday School By The Owner's Design

100 Tools
For Successful
Kingdom Growth

Danny Von Kanel

CSS Publishing Company, Inc., Lima, Ohio

Copyright © 2005 by
CSS Publishing Company, Inc.
Lima, Ohio

Scripture quotations are from the King James Version of the Bible, in the public domain.

Library of Congress Cataloging-in-Publication Data

Von Kanel, Danny, 1955-
  Building Sunday school by the owner's design : 100 Tools for building successful
Kingdom growth / Danny Von Kanel.
      p. cm.
  ISBN 0-7880-2353-5 (perfect bound : alk. paper)
  1. Christian education of adults. 2. Sunday schools—growth. I. Title.

  BV1550.V36 2005
  268—dc22

                                                                    2005004461

For more information about CSS Publishing Company resources, visit our website at
www.csspub.com or e-mail us at custserv@csspub.com or call (800) 241-4056.

ISBN 0-7880-2353-5   PRINTED IN U.S.A.

*I dedicate this book
to the memory of my mother,
Madge Click Von Kanel*

and

*to the memory of my nephew,
Landon Von Kanel*

Acknowledgments

To my wife, Beverly, who has been everything I wanted in a wife ... and much, much more.

To my sons, Allen and Brad, who have enriched my life beyond measure and have given me reasons to continue to write.

To Barbara A. Robidoux for her critiquing skills and unique way of encouraging me to always have hope in my writing potential.

To Marie Wascom for her gifted editing skills and for accepting to do this "gargantuan favor."

To Luther Sanford, III, for being my pastor and for showing me how much I still have to learn about building the Sunday school.

To Jonathon Smith, Stan Purdum, Missy Cotrell, and all the CSS Publishing staff for believing in me and for making this book a wonderful reality.

To my two "true-blue" fans, Charlotte Spencer and Anita McNeal, for always going the extra mile in ministry and for giving encouragement.

To all my "raving fans," most of whom belong to the Sweet Spirit Singers in Liberty, Mississippi, I say, "Thank you" for four-and-one-half wonderful years as your director. If Sunday school could be grown by singing, you would have brought it about with grace.

Table Of Contents

Chapter 1

Why Build Sunday School By The Owner's Design?

The Christian church in America is in the midst of a major downturn in growth. Eighty percent of churches deal weekly with plateau and decline. With the population in Canada and the United States at 338 million, only 78 million claim to be Christian. Church attendance has dropped by 11 percent. Though Sunday school was once revered in the '50s as the catalyst for outreach, it has in many places become a by-gone program that has lost its punch.

According to Barna Research, "Adult Sunday school classes ranked in the middle ground of those things that influenced their decision of whether or not to return to a church they had visited. Only 26 percent ranked it as extremely important, while 23 percent listed it as pretty important and 30 percent somewhat important. It ranked ninth out of 22 factors."[1]

Could it be that Sunday school has lost its influence because classes have become a reservoir for depositing head knowledge without emphasizing life change and application?

Church growth is anything done that produces life change, kingdom growth in numbers, and deeply committed followers of Christ. Some growing churches spend thousands of dollars on marketing. High profile Christian leaders surf the preaching channels, and acts designed to draw in people produce large crowds, opulent cathedrals, and growth magnification in these churches.

But most church leaders don't have such resources. They have to use what tools they have available. They have to employ tools that use time, energy, and their God-given imagination to maximize Sunday school to its fullest.

Owner's Design vs. Traditional
And/Or Contemporary Church Growth

What are the characteristics of building the church by the Owner's Design as compared to traditional and/or contemporary church growth? Owner's Design church growth differs in six ways:

1. Church growth practices among traditional churches are time constrained. Owner's Design growth precepts are in step with the master timekeeper.

2. Church growth rationale amid contemporary churches is no sure ticket to ministry involvement growth. Owner's Design growth principles maximize spiritual gifts and place a high premium on using gifts through ministry participation.

3. Church growth in traditional churches uses programs that replace evangelism. Owner's Design thinking assures that evangelism is enhanced.

4. Church growth in contemporary churches uses marketing to meet felt needs. Owner's Design growth planning involves meeting real needs.

5. Church growth in traditional churches attempts to start new programs that struggle to function in a maintenance mode and

8

find acceptance in an unchanging bureaucracy. Owner's Design growth comes about because new programs are started only after an old, unproductive one is ended.

6. Contemporary church growth advocates targeting one audience in the community. Owner's Design growth recommends targeting all audiences — finding ways to reach all segments of society in their locale.

The Six Most Important Sunday School Secrets

Sunday school classes ... encourage people to share their hurts, find help, and provide a safe place to hear the clear message of the gospel. — Dr. Alvin L. Reid

1. Steering — *Sunday school works in reaching people when the pastor leads out in its promotion, outreach, and planning.*

Pastors don't have to have ultimate control, but they must stay involved — providing leadership, guidance, and inspiration. Pastors who talk, sleep, eat, and dream Sunday school have Sunday schools that are a priority. In most churches, when the pastor speaks, the people listen. What's important to church leadership becomes important to the congregation. Significance breeds potential for involvement and growth.

2. Serving — *Sunday school teachers who have a servant heart reap class members who model the same. Such teachers move beyond serving their class and into the marketplace.*

Life-giving churches are empowered by worshipers who willingly invest their lives in life-giving ministry.
— Gary L. McIntosh

Sunday schools that connect with their community through meeting real needs always capture the hearts of people. Teachers are key to such shaping of hearts and minds, though inwardly developed servanthood is outwardly demonstrated. Teaching for life

9

transformation ultimately leads those remade to go share Jesus through servant actions and spoken testimony.

3. **Sowing** — *Sunday school classes grow when they scatter seeds of outreach and ministry. Constant sowing is the norm. Multiple means are the tools used.*

Growing classes always have prospect lists that are continually worked. Ministry projects are consistently planned and implemented. Such classes understand that growth is hard work but recognize the necessity. They readily grasp the sowing/reaping principle: if no seeds are sown, no fruit can be expected.

Such sowing among growing churches is recognized as evangelism. Sunday school is vital to that concept. "We know that people's behavior is driven by their beliefs, and the research showed that the most significant distinction between those who share Christ with the culture, and those who don't relates to their religious beliefs."[2]

4. **Shaping** — *Growing Sunday school classes fully intend to shape lives — what they expect to do, they do. Non-growing Sunday school classes don't.*

Growing classes expect equipping to take place. "To equip means to prepare, to dress, to array, to outfit. The ancients used the word to mean setting a dislocated joint, putting it in order."[3] Such shaping doesn't happen by chance. A plan for these churches is set in motion to bring about the desired results. Nongrowing Sunday schools expect nothing and get just that every time. They don't expect what they don't plan.

5. **Spreading** — *Growing Sunday schools recognize that new classes must constantly be started.*

Ultimately, this means some members leave their ranks in order to provide a nucleus for the new class. They don't fight the concept. They identify such losses as decisive gains for their church and God's kingdom. Such classes place more importance on growing the body of Christ than keeping their class intact.

This spreading concept is possible when church leaders share how classes can reproduce themselves. Class extensions, though functioning as a new class, are really a mirror image that grew out of the parent class.

6. **Studying** — *The Bible is the textbook for all growing Sunday schools.*

Though supplementary materials are used and are varied, the Bible is promoted, used, and remains primary. Sunday schools in some mainline denominations that have embraced the New Age movement, by steering members away from God's Word or minimizing its significance, have all struggled to keep from decline.

God blesses those Sunday schools that keep Christ and his Word the primary focus. Why would he bless anything else?

Sunday School Wisdom

The most prolific North American Protestant group, the Southern Baptists, credits its growth not only to divinely empowered preaching built on evangelistic theology, but also its system of Sunday school organization that gives lay-people a very significant role as lay ministers.[4]

Creative roles are still available through the Sunday school ministry. Put an Owner's Design spin on them and watch for empowered lay people.

Building Sunday school by the Owner's (God's) Design is the surest way to successful kingdom growth. Varied in makeup, key components comprise the design. All Sunday schools, using a plethora of methods, keep Christ and his Word uppermost. Those who keep their lifeline to Christ flowing, employ the creativity and supernatural energy of our Lord. These Sunday schools keep people in the forefront and see their Sunday school ministry as a tool to accomplish the task.

Such reasons should prompt all churches to decide to build Sunday school by the Owner's Design. Once the decision is made, the church can gain valuable help in beginning this process by using the church leader's guide for ministry (in the next chapter) ... for such a time as this.

----

1. George Barna, Barna Research. Internet online. Available from <www.barna. org/FlexPage.aspx?Page+Topic+TopicID=9> 1999.

2. George Barna, Barna Research. Internet online. Available from <www.barna. org/FlexPage.aspx?Page=BarnaUpdate+BarnaUpdateID=14> [July 28, 2003].

3. Charles A. Tidwell, *Church Administration: Effective Leadership for Ministry* (Nashville, Tennessee: Broadman Press, 1985), p. 28.

4. Carl F. George, *Prepare Your Church for the Future* (Grand Rapids, Michigan: Revell, 1992), p. 28.

Chapter 2

A Church Leader's Guide To Ministry ... For Such A Time As This

Sunday school, as lived out in most of today's churches, has become a non-effective program. Without some serious refocusing on its purpose and re-energizing it through effective tools, Sunday school will cease to be as we know it, or it will continue in name only. What began as an effective ministry, falling within God's design, has degraded into a program that propagates transferring head knowledge instead of life change. Such degeneration must change.

I want to guide you in moving beyond such a program focus to a ministry that is enlivened. It begins with understanding, verbalizing, and educating our lay leaders about some basic truths of Sunday school.

Basic Truths

1. Sunday school's basic function is to bring about life change, not transfer head knowledge. Evangelism creates evangelizers through the Sunday school. "In a typical week, evangelizers

(are) more likely to attend a Sunday school class (42 percent - 22 percent)."[1]

2. The pastor is the catalyst for a life change focus in the church — such a focus bleeds over into every ministry, including Sunday school.

3. The teacher is the medium for transformation in the classroom.

4. A variety of Sunday school tools must be used simultaneously for overall impact.

5. A personal quiet time emphasis must permeate the church body. Daily personal intimacy with God softens hearts to be receptive to change when God's Word is taught during Sunday school.

6. An outreach focus should supersede an inward mentality and focus.

Moving beyond these basic truths are some underlying applications that are extremely practical in nature:

1. The pastor provides personal application in his sermons and gives actions to complete over the coming week to live out the truth(s) of the message.

2. Every Sunday school lesson ends with personal application — an asking of class members to do something specific during the coming week to live out what they have learned.

3. Every teacher models the weekly concept taught and is the first to report on the results of living out the truth. The teacher fully understands that "Sunday school classes can encourage people to share their hurts, find help, and provide a safe place to hear the clear message of the gospel."[2]

4. A conscious attempt is made to live out 72 of the 100 tools

given in this book — simultaneously as much as possible.

5. Outreach is made a habit. Every week, time is made for out-reach planning — making use of every conceivable tool available sometime during the year. Evangelism is the thrust.

6. Through visuals, announcements, and testimonies, a personal quiet time is kept as a priority in the church.

All the tools given are meant to assist you in building Sunday school by the Owner's Design. Use each tool and watch these basic truths and practical principles be lived out in your church through the Sunday school.

---

1. George Barna, Barna Research. Internet online. Available from <www.barna.org/FlexPage.aspx?Page=Barnaupdate+BarnaUpdateID=147> [July 28, 2003].

2. Alvin Reid, *Radically Unchurched* (Grand Rapids, Michigan: Kregel Publications, 2002), p. 140.

Chapter 3

The Most Dynamic Leadership Tools Available To Church Leaders

*I want the whole Christ for my Savior, the whole Bible
for my book, the whole church for my fellowship, and
the whole world for my mission field.*[1]
— John Wesley

Throughout Christian history, certain tools have always impacted the church in powerful ways. Most we use but don't fully recognize their significance. When we have employed these implements, we haven't considered them in regard to Sunday school. Each carries the respect of the congregation without having utilized the tool to impact Sunday school.

When we channel the full force of these tools toward revitalizing, re-igniting, and refocusing the ministry of Sunday school, the sky is the limit for positive results taking place.

1. God (Free) — Our Most Powerful Resource

Obvious? Not Exactly. Most congregations would be offended if God was left out of the picture; yet, most implement Sunday school as if he didn't exist. The creator of the universe is at our disposal for guidance, direction, and empowering. If he can speak the world into existence, surely he can fill teaching positions, motivate workers, enable outreach, and multiply attendance in Sunday school. We have not because we ask not.

The God who inspired writers to pen the words, "Thy Word is sharper than any two-edged sword" and "Study to shew thyself approved under God" will also enable the one ministry designed to teach his Word to flourish. But he won't force his way into our well-laid plans. He will lead and guide when asked.

Consider answering the following:
- Where does God fit into our plans for Sunday school?
- How do our prayers reflect God's involvement?
- When was the last time we asked God to empower all that we do in Sunday school?

2. You (Free)

No one understands Sunday school like you. Your energy, personality, gifts, and desire to make Sunday school prosper is unsurpassed. You wouldn't be reading this book if that weren't so.

One of the main reasons for Sunday schools' decline across our nation is because leaders have quit leading. Now it's time for them to step up, reclaim their roles, and never look back. It's time to marshall their skills for the task and promote Bible study like only they can. Let the congregation see their passion for Bible study through the Sunday school.

Always remember: If you won't carry the Sunday school banner, who will? And even if someone else is more available, they probably lack the skill, passion, resolve, and the respect of the congregation to bring out the best in Sunday school.

3. Pastor (Free)

Half the battle is won when a pastor embraces Sunday school with heart, body, mind, and soul. Congregations tend to place importance on what the pastor sees as a priority.

The pastor offers leadership that no other single person in the church body can give. As a full-time Minister of Music and Education, I've learned that my words carried weight only when they were backed by a pastor's words and actions. I'm reminded of an old television commercial: "When E.F. Hutton speaks, everyone listens." When the pastor speaks, everyone listens. A pastor speaking and living Sunday school will empower people to embrace the ministry with unwavering devotion and support.

4. Deacons (Free)

In regard to the SBC FAITH program, my former pastor said, "If a large majority of the deacon body doesn't become personally involved with this program, it will die on the vine in three years."

Such can be said of the Sunday school. Deacons must lead out in support of the Sunday school — every deacon a member — every deacon actively and verbally lending support. Congregations notice deacons who serve. They appreciate and follow deacons who wholeheartedly embrace Sunday school.

5. Sunday School/Small Group Leaders (Free)

Sunday school or small group classes will rise or fall based on the quality of the teacher/facilitator. A spiritually gifted teacher who loves God and people with his/her whole heart, and who is committed to bringing about life change, will produce a class that reproduces itself ten times over.

The pastor and staff mobilize such teachers by:
• Identifying spiritual gifts
• Nurturing spiritual intimacy
• Modeling life change

> *There is no greater investment in the future of the church than by identifying, encouraging, and providing training for young leaders in our midst. It's something every church can do!* — Robert Lewis

6. Congregation (Free)

Most congregations will follow when the pastor and staff/elder board/presbytery lead. When the entire congregation is mobilized to carry out the task of Sunday school, a community can be set on fire for the study of God's Word. The church leadership task is to equip the saints. When equipping takes place, the multiplication principle kicks in. Growing numbers begin to flood our Sunday school classes with new units having to be formed.

As church leadership nurtures spiritual intimacy and models life change, starting new units becomes a means to carry out the Great Commission and not a battle for classes who fear losing class members to the new starts.

Tool Time
Avoid the perception of splitting a class
- Begin a class from scratch by using present non-attendees as a starting class roll.
- Launch a major media blitz and outreach program to secure members for a new class.
- Discuss with the present class the idea that a new class would be an extension of the existing class. Request that some of the members be missionaries for the new start.

7. Staff (Free)
Staff, in this case, refers to other God-called ministers who assist the senior pastor in the work of ministry. They are indispensable in keeping the wheels of Sunday school running.

The staff is responsible for keeping Sunday school in the forefront of lay leaders and the congregation. They assist in staffing, training, encouragement, and outreach.

The key to keeping staff members pumped about Sunday school is to award their efforts, give pay raises, affirm publicly, and allow them to pursue their dreams. A loving pastor in good times and bad will assure a staff that will enthusiastically embrace a pastor's leadership of the Sunday school.

Tool Time

Questioning staff

A key question every pastor should ask staff is, "What can I do to help you reach your dreams for your area of Sunday school?" When staff responds, do your best to do as they request!

---

1. John Wesley, source unknown.

Chapter 4

The Most Dynamic Tools In
Developing Spiritual Disciplines

> *We must face the fact that many today are notoriously careless in their living. This attitude finds its way into the church. We have liberty, we have money, we live in comparative luxury. As a result, discipline has practically disappeared. What would a violin sound like if the strings on the musician's instrument were all hanging loose, not stretched tight, not "disciplined"?*
> — A. W. Tozer, *Men Who Met God*

Spiritual disciplines help resonate life when they permeate the Sunday school. Anemic Christians are ill-suited to carry out the tasks of Sunday school: reach, teach, witness, minister, fellowship, and worship. Weak quiet times foster feeble students. Consistent personal worship failure leaves classes unable to hear God when he speaks. We must nurture these disciplines so that all class members are maturing daily — ready to hear God speak through their teacher on Sundays. These disciplines each serve as tools to

23

tighten the strings of our lives so that we may produce the beautiful music of fruitful lives God intended. They are: prayer, Bible study, personal quiet time, fasting, journaling, and worship.

8. Prayer (Free)

I have found prayer to be very effective. "At a national conference, I heard about a church that tested the effectiveness of prayer. They identified eighty homes and prayed for those homes for ninety days. After ninety days, witnessing teams were dispatched to those homes as well as to eighty homes that had received no prayer support. Of the eighty homes that had received no focused prayer, only one family invited them in. Of the eighty homes that received the ninety days of prayer, 67 welcomed the teams! Prayer matters."[1] And many Americans believe in prayer: "81 percent of adults out of 176 pray to God."

Prayer is important to the churches surveyed in my 2003 BSSQ survey; 66 percent said their church was somewhat successful or very successful in developing the spiritual disciplines of prayer and Bible study. Only 5 percent said their church was poor in this area.

Successful prayer development can be modeled by teachers for their students. Beyond the ordinary praying at the beginning and ending of class, a teacher can place supreme importance on prayer by asking for prayer concerns and listening intensely with a heart of empathy and concern. Followed by a heartfelt prayer for each request, the student senses the teacher truly cares and prayer is his/her means to finding answers and getting help. "Implementing an intentional prayer strategy through your Sunday school (*class*) will impact the church's corporate prayer life and ministry."[2]

A teacher who prays regularly and intensely with class members will reap a class that prays through the week. Opportunities to pray with members outside the classroom further amplifies that windfall. A prayed-up class will come to Sunday school with a heart overflowing for God — ready to get their marching orders for the coming week. This discipline must be discussed, studied, modeled, used, promoted, and relied upon — making the class its own house of prayer in the larger body of corporate classes.

Tool Resource

Excellent tool on prayer

Power House (A Step-By-Step Guide To Building A Church That Prays), by Glen Martin and Dian Ginter, is a unique tool that is applicable to individual Sunday school classes.

9. Personal Bible Study (Low Cost)

Why study the Bible during the week? Why isn't Sunday Bible study enough? Try going a week without your spouse talking to you! Not much fun is it? We speak to God through prayer. He talks to us through the scriptures. Daily speaking begets daily intimacy. Daily intimacy reaps a tender heart that is used to God speaking. Bring together a body of tender hearts on a given Sunday and watch for spiritual overflow in the classroom and into the worship arena.

In our 2003 BSSQ survey, 35 percent of the respondents said their church was adequate or poor in developing the spiritual discipline of personal Bible study — 14 percent very successful and 52 percent somewhat successful. If these statistics hold true, we can feel reasonably good about our accomplishments in this area.

The minimal cost of this tool comes in the form of extra study materials such as a Bible dictionary, concordance, and commentary — though none are absolutely necessary in understanding the scriptures. I know that runs contrary to the theological elite, but really, the Holy Spirit is our guide. In saying that, let me add that most of our study would benefit from these helps.

Tool Time

Keys to a quality lesson
- **A Catching Hook** — This opening may be in the form of a shocking illustration, a recent community happening, a pertinent statistic, or real-life testimony. Present it with excitement, energy, and enthusiasm.
- **A Convincing Heart** — Share how you were first convinced by the scriptural truth. Bring the passage back to the class by asking, "Now what are you going to do? Are you convinced of this scripture's truth?"

- **A Contagious Habit** — Look for truths the class can practice. Determine a specific action to do. Enlist accountability partners. Share results. Continuous practice develops a habit. Habits by a few can become contagious.

10. Personal Quiet Time (Free)

Quiet Time
by Tina English
In the morning there's a special time when I sit and talk to God. Not a quick hello or a cry for help, but in prayer and thanks I come. He is always seated there, waiting in the parlor of my heart. There he speaks to me, reminding me of him I am a part. My quiet time with God to get to know him better; My quiet hour with him to learn to love him more.

When you combine prayer and Bible study in a daily concentrated period of time, you have a quiet time. Quiet times can include other tools in the form of fasting, journaling, and worship.

Personal quiet times provide Sunday school class members the opportunity for greater intimacy with God. As God is allowed to break into their worlds, class members see God for who he is and themselves for who they are in Christ. In essence, in every quiet time there is the potential for class members to become more Christlike.

Can you see how this would impact a class? Fewer hindrances to the reception of God's Word would allow for greater transformation of lives. All because of personal quiet times.

Tool Time
Quiet time guidelines
- Try to start your day with your quiet time.
- Find a location free of interruptions and distractions.
- Use scripture reading and prayer to start with. Add scripture memory, meditation, journaling, fasting, and worship over a period of time.

- If you must miss, commit to start back the next day.
- If possible, secure a partner to keep you accountable.

11. Fasting (Free)

Defraud ye not one the other, except it be with consent for a time, that ye may give yourselves to fasting and prayer. — 1 Corinthians 7:5

Fasting is a special time when you allow your body to go without nourishment in order to focus on the things of God. Such decisions to fast are between the one fasting and God. Neither the Sunday school teacher nor other class members should know about the one fasting, unless health issues are involved. Fasting should be for special times when class members need answers on serious issues or want to take their spiritual walk to a new level.

The state of one's health should always be considered before entering a time of extended fasting. If no one else is told, one's physician should be made aware before entering a fasting period.

Fasting is not a common practice among the churches who took the 2003 BSSQ survey: 29 percent said they never engage in the discipline, 52 percent some of the time, 5 percent participate in fasting all the time, and 10 percent most of the time.

Fasting is a unique tool God has given us to allow our minds, bodies, and spirits to focus on him. Giant leaps in spiritual maturity have happened when class members have fasted — giving their hearts, minds, bodies, and souls to the Lord.

12. Journaling (Free)

Journaling is a unique way that Sunday school members can express their thoughts and actions and record their personal journeys with the Lord.

For many folks, this takes the form of writing out prayers. Great encouragement comes from looking back and seeing how God answered our prayers expressed in a journal.

Journaling also is not a common practice among churches who took the 2003 BSSQ survey: 81 percent never engage in this discipline, or only do so some of the time.

Yet, records of our spiritual walk have a way of staying with us longer. As members have opportunity and are comfortable sharing, they provide unique vignettes that can be shared to encourage other class members. Journaling can be made a part of a personal quiet time or can be done separately.

Tool Time

Journaling — a spiritual discipline

"If you've never kept a spiritual journal, or have given up on journaling, try these suggestions.

- Think outside the lines — Creativity is the name of the game.
- Forget grammar — Don't even write in complete sentences if you don't want to. Jot down phrases, words, scriptures, or quotes.
- Keep it under wraps — Keep your journal in a safe place. A journal is most effective when you're completely honest in your expressions. You'll feel better able to candidly express your deepest thoughts and longings if you know your roommate or spouse won't accidentally see your journal.
- Accentuate the positive — Don't focus on the negative. Some people only feel like expressing themselves when they're upset, angry, or depressed."[3]

13. Worship (Free)

This tool uses all of the above tools in combination or separately. They are expressed in private worship. Every time we read God's Word, pray, engage in a personal quiet time, write in a journal, or fast, worship should be the outcome.

Corporate worship is also a necessary tool for class members to express their gratitude and love — to see evangelism take place. "Religion never evangelized anybody. Yet, if Christ is not the focal point of our worship, that is all we have — religion."[4]

The Sunday school hour should be an overflow from private worship of Christ that spills over from the class into focused co-operate worship.

Tool Time

Personal techniques

Private worship has taken on new meaning when I have:
• read the Psalms, substituting personal pronouns to personalize the psalms,
• sung songs that I knew were straight scripture or a paraphrase,
• spent considerable time meditating on a particular scripture, and
• written out my prayers.

Tools 9-14 lead to depth for any Sunday school class. The more that Sunday school class members engage in these spiritual disciplines, the more spiritually dynamic our classes. Nothing can replace daily experiences with the Lord.

----

1. Alvin Reid, *Radically Unchurched* (Grand Rapids, Michigan: Kregal Publications, 2002), p. 50.

2. John H. Ewart, *The Journal of the American Society for Church Growth, The Intentional Sunday School: A Pathway to Purpose*, Vol. 14, Winter, 2003, p. 21.

3. Christian Fellowship Church, Youth Zone. Internet online. Available from <www.cfc-net.org/journaling.htm>.

4. Sally Morgenthaler, *Worship Evangelism* (Grand Rapids, Michigan: Zondervan, 1999), p. 109.

Chapter 5

The Most Dynamic Tools In Growing
Sunday Schools Through Outreach

*It is easy to determine when something is aflame. It
ignites other material. Any fire that does not spread
will eventually go out. A church without evangelism is
a contradiction in terms, just as a fire that does not
burn is a contradiction.*   — Bruce L. Shelley,
                        Christian Theology In Plain Language

Sunday school dies or thrives on how well it does outreach
and evangelism. When a number of outreach tools are used in combination, the greater the benefit. The following tools have proven
effective in reaching people without a great amount of cost. Though
outreach is hard work, it is made easier when it is shared by each
class member.

14. Weekly Visitation (Free)
    Weekly visitation gives a class the opportunity to reach out,
not only to class members, but to new people in the community.

Also, according to staff member Robert Dillard at Coral Ridge Presbyterian Church of Fort Lauderdale, Florida, "It is difficult to imagine any effective growth ... without weekly ... following up visitors."[1] Though speaking of his church, this truth equally applies to us all.

New additions always impact a class and create excitement. Visitation should be done on the same night of the week and at the same time. Tying the weekly visitation to fulfilling the Great Commission is a key ingredient to motivating class members. How often visitation is held, weekly or monthly, should be based on the size of your community and potential prospects.

Though alive and well in 53 percent of churches (2003 BSSQ), 43 percent of churches do not have a visitation program. Of those who do, 23 percent have weekly visitation; 19 percent monthly; 5 percent quarterly, and 5 percent irregularly. The key to their success was having quality prospects.

Hot prospects are those who visit your church for the first time. Within 24 hours, someone from your class or church needs to be in those homes. Gary McIntosh gives five principles of follow-up when making contacts: "1) A friendly contact, 2) A personal contact, 3) A prompt contact, 4) A non-threatening contact, and 5) A continual contact."[2]

Class outreach is further enhanced when it is a part of a total church effort in visitation. No class is an island. Each is a part of the larger church family, the body of Christ. Every effort should be made to participate in the church sanctioned night for visitation, if it has one. If not, your class is free to set its own day and time.

Tool Time

Priority visitation

The key to making visitation a priority in your class and church is to have church leaders affirm the night of church-wide visitation and not allow any other church activity to be scheduled on that night.

15. Forty Men And Forty Women For God On Visitation

This creative tool is one that any size church can use to help Sunday school classes reach out through visitation. I have used this approach on several occasions with the same results.

- **Issue the challenge** — On a Sunday morning, a month prior to the next monthly visitation night, issue a challenge to your people that God wants forty men and forty women to commit to visit on Monday night of the next visitation.
- **Promote the event** — Print a commitment form and place it in your Sunday school records each week to promote the visitation night. As people commit to visit, print their names under the heading, "Forty Men And Forty Women For God On Visitation," in your church newsletter. In addition, make a computer-generated wall display, listing each person's name, and tape the names to the wall. (Note: People like seeing their names in print.)
- **Prepare for the night** — Prepare visitation cards. If God is in forty men and forty women going visiting, he will provide the large number of prospects. If prospects are not readily available, use an ongoing telephone survey, lists of new utility users, vacation Bible school prospects, and people in your church who are church members only.
- **Come expecting** — Help your people to expect more than eighty in attendance. When they come, distribute visitation cards, thank them for coming, and pray thanking God for the turnout. Then send them out two by two. You can reasonably expect 125 contacts to be made inviting people to Sunday school.

16. GROW — Outreach Teams That Win (Low Cost)

I am presently using the GROW program at my church. This program was designed by Jerry Tidwell, pastor of West Jackson Baptist Church, Jackson, Tennessee. The outreach we are accomplishing has been impressive. GROW is based on five principles: 1) Sowing and reaping, 2) Involving every member, 3) Having fun with outreach, 4) Making quality time greater than quantity time, and 5) Reaching out by divine appointment.

GROW works with four teams — G, R, O, and W. Church members volunteer to serve on a team and do one of three things:

call people by telephone, write letters, or visit. Resource material is available that includes training videos and a disk with printable forms, or by accessing <www.lifeway.com> online.

17. FAITH (Low Cost)

A more advanced system of reaching people through the Sunday school is the Faith Sunday School Evangelism Strategy. FAITH is an ongoing, comprehensive process which functions through the existing Sunday school. FAITH equips and mobilizes Sunday school classes to accomplish these ministry "touches."

• Personal Evangelism/Soul Winning
• Follow-up on new believers
• Assimilation/Discipleship
• Reclaiming absentees
• Ministry to regular attendees

Crossing denominational lines, this tool has been used to equip pastors and church leaders in over 6,500 churches since 1998. This can be ordered online, also, at <www.lifeway.com>.

18. Outreach Leaders (Free)

Outreach leaders, if carefully selected, can be a tremendous help to any class' efforts at reaching people. If it is just a name to fill a position, you'd be better off not having one. The outreach leader should be a self-starter — one who loves people and has a passion to see others brought into Christ's kingdom.

Class outreach leaders should serve for one year. If they do a good job, they should be asked to continue.

Responsibilities include making visitation assignments, keeping an up-to-date prospect list, and leading out in all visitation efforts.

19. Telephone Calls/Letters/Postcards (Low Cost)

Church growth experts tell us that by calling everyone on your Sunday school roll, you can increase your attendance by 20 percent for the next Sunday. Letters work best when they come from the pastor the week before a high-attendance day or Sunday school campaign. Postcards are cost efficient and can be sent weekly.

A weekly outreach plan that works is alternating these three with personal visits. For instance:
- Week 1 — Personal visit
- Week 2 — Telephone call
- Week 3 — Letter
- Week 4 — Postcard

Such an outreach approach reveals what Reverend Jerry Falwell calls the "Two secret weapons of a Bible believing local church: 1) contacting people, and 2) contacting people continuously. If you do that long enough, well enough, and loud enough, you are going to get everyone's attention."[3]

A class secretary can prepare absentee postcards when they finish the records or can do them at home. Limit mailings to the home to one a week. Coordination with church staff may be needed in order to avoid flooding Sunday school class members with mail from various ministries.

20. Home Bible Study (Low Cost)

People will come to a home more quickly than they will to a church facility. Classes are not limited by a time frame or a location. Reaching the lost is done best by inviting people in your neighborhood to yours or your member's homes.

"Most people who are opposed to the gospel are not opposed to ice cream."[4] Plan a party, invite the lost, teach God's Word, and you will reap a whirlwind of saved souls. Pray, plan, promote, and preach — and let the Holy Spirit work.

Homes work extremely well with teenagers. I set up what we called Lifestyle meetings in eight different homes led by older teens and college-age young adults. I had been ministering to about forty teens at church. The first Thursday night of our meetings, we had ninety teens turn out. By the end of the thirteenth week, we had 135 teenagers in attendance ... and this was on a school night.

> *No more room at church. Home Bible study is the perfect solution for space problems.*

21. Community Awareness Evangelism (Low Cost)

This is the GOING of the Great Commission. The days are over when people will come to our Sunday school classes just by seeing our buildings on the corner. People, as observers, want to know we care. We do so by being creative with the kinds of activities we offer to meet real needs of people. To use this strategy of outreach, you'll want to Generate a needs list in the community, Organize the project to meet the need, Initiate the project, Nail down follow-up plans, and Gravitate those at the end of the follow-up back to a new beginning of the same project.

A more detailed description of this tool is found in chapter 7 of my book, *Built By The Owner's Design: The Positive Approach To Building Your Church God's Way.*

22. Conversion Evangelism (Low Cost)

This is the *baptizing* them section of the Great Commission. It is the conscious effort of seeking to win to Christ those we have identified through community awareness evangelism. Through the gospel presentation we allow the Holy Spirit to make followers of Christ. The strategy includes going to the "lost sheep" (Matthew 10:6), preaching or declaring the "gospel" (Matthew 10:7), ministering "freely" (Matthew 10:8), and being "wise and harmless" (Matthew 10:16).

The tool actively engages Sunday school members to share their faith. Research shows we're lacking in this area. "Slightly less than one out of four adults who attend a Protestant church (23 percent) are both born again in their faith and have shared their faith in Jesus Christ with a non-Christian in the past twelve months."[5]

A more descriptive look at this tool can be found in chapter 8 of *Built By The Owner's Design.*

23. Comprehension Evangelism (Low Cost)

This is the *teaching all nations* section of the Great Commission. It is the concerted effort to move the new convert into the fellowship of a small group, thereby becoming a learner. The strategy will be to team them with a mature Christian, enlist them in a new-members' class, access an "in touch" plan, capture the class spirit for the new convert, and help them progress past spiritual infancy.

More details to this tool can be found in chapter 9 of *Built By The Owner's Design*.

24. Confirmation Evangelism (Low Cost)

This is the *making disciples* section of the Great Commission. It is the progression from spiritual infancy to spiritual maturity. This strategy develops spiritual growth prerequisites in the areas of Bible study, prayer, worship, fellowship, and the sharing of one's faith. This completed structure leads Sunday school class members to be doers, reproducing followers, and leading others to maturity in Christ.

Further explanation of this tool is available in my book, *Built By The Owner's Design*, in chapter 10.

Outreach and evangelism is an ongoing process. Daily, weekly, monthly, and yearly efforts ... year after year ... reap results — results that can be measured by numbers and by continuous spiritual maturity of those involved.

1. Danny Von Kanel, *Journal for the American Society for Church Growth*, "Assimilation: The Touch, See, and Hear Approach," Vol. 14, Winter 2003, p. 36.

2. Gary McIntosh, *The Exodus Principle* (Nashville, Tennessee: Broadman Holman, 1995), p. 165.

3. Jerry Falwell, *Journal for the American Society for Church Growth*, "I Still Believe In Saturation Evangelism," Vol. 14, Winter, 2003, p. 9.

4. Josh Hunt, *You Can Double Your Class in Two Years or Less* (Loveland, Colorado: Group Publishing, 1997), p. 63.

5. George Barna, Barna Research. Internet online. Available from <www.barna.org/FlexPage.aspx?Page=BarnaUpdate&BarnaUpdateID=14> [July 28, 2003].

Chapter 6

Tools That Are
Qualities Of Growth

Growing Sunday schools across the world are distinguished by certain characteristics. These tools represent qualities of growth. The more apropos the qualities manifested by Sunday schools in these churches, the greater the growth. We must answer the question: Do our Sunday schools exhibit these qualities? Once answered, we can address areas of weakness and strive to maximize our strengths.

25. Excellence (Free)
Mediocrity in Sunday school undermines use of the previous 24 growth tools. If our nation's financial systems were run with the same poor standards, economic ruin would surely follow.

Individual Sunday school classes cannot settle for ordinariness. Excellence must encompass all we do. "Highly effective churches establish high standards to which they are held accountable — of their own volition. The churches set high expectations for their students and plan to meet those expectations."[1] This degree of quality starts with the teacher.

If you are a Sunday school/small group teacher or facilitator, let me suggest you get the best training possible. Modify your teaching methods. If you use the lecture method continuously, consider trying something different. The comment, "I'm bored," is still the number one reason people give for not liking their Sunday school class.

The teachers I know who impacted my life in Sunday school and in my public education were those who desired and were committed to excellence.

26. Simplicity (Free)

Simplicity eliminates obstacles to class participation. Class members gravitate toward class involvement when they feel accepted and know that what is being asked of them is simple to say, do, or be.

Class members' knowledge of the Bible is diverse. Some know the books of the Bible and can find them quickly. Others have no prior knowledge. Simplify finding passages. Avoid intimidating members in any way. If you ask for class participation, make sure they understand what you are asking and how to use the method of delivery.

Tool Time

Three-step rule

Make requests of class members using the three-step rule: "If it takes more than three steps to do, don't use it."

27. Consistency (Free)

Sunday school class members long to see consistency from teachers. Be a teacher who does what he or she says. Be consistent in season and out of season.

If you tend to be moody, work on controlling your mood swings. Class members approach teachers with their hurts when they don't have to guess what mood their teacher is in. Examine your life in light of scripture. Your class needs to see a teacher's life in step with scripture. A modeled consistent life tends to re-produce the same.

As a ten-year-old, I remember Gloria Clark, who lived out her faith when she was the department director of our older children's Sunday school department. Her consistent living and love of our age group was vivid to all who came in touch with her. My life and the lives of others around her were forever changed by her influence. She indeed was a consistent example — in good times and bad — for cancer ultimately took her from us.

28. Accountability (Free)

Accountability builds Sunday schools by keeping goals, actions, and attitudes on track. Outreach suffers when classes are allowed to set their own agendas. A teacher who teaches should also be one who reaches out to others. Leadership must consistently be encouraging, reminding, and addressing outreach needs.

Class members fulfill lessons learned when they have an accountability partner encouraging and helping them to walk straight. Such a partner who prays, corrects, rebukes, and encourages is a lifesaver when faced with a life-changing choice.

29. Love (Free)

Sunday school classes prosper when every member knows he or she is loved by other members. Love attracts. Love will overcome a lot of class shortcomings. Stressing participation in the spiritual disciplines in tools 8 to 13 is the best way to strengthen the class love quotient. The more we love our Lord, the more we will love his people.

God forbid that you have classes with people who not only don't love but also don't like one another. It may be time to see each one separately and then together to get at the heart of the matter. Do it prayerfully. Do it redemptively. Forgiveness and reconciliation by two members who others know have been at odds is a powerful demonstration of God's power — and that will definitely impact the class.

Class love quotient

On a scale of 1-10, access your class love quotient:

1. Class members really know each other. _____

2. Class members show weekly concern for absentees. _____

3. Class members are there for each other during times of crisis. _____

4. Class members have great empathy for each other. They cry when others cry, laugh when they laugh. _____

5. Class members say "I love you" to each other. _____

6. Class members have demonstrated a willingness to forgive. _____

Score: 55-60 — High quality and quantity of love

45-54 — Class loves but needs improvement

35-44 — Class lacks a loving, cohesive relationship

6-34 — Major work needed to improve love quotient

30. Creativity (Free)

I'm convinced the reason mediocrity embraces so many Sunday schools is because teachers have left their creativity outside the classroom door. Most of us are more creative than we think. Turning a scripture passage into a dramatic skit, monologue, or musical presentation is within all of us. Role playing a modern-day situation to illustrate a spiritual truth, placing chairs facing corners of a room to illustrate people who feel alienated from society, or playing a game of Jeopardy using biblical topics are creative ways to teach.

Life change instead of teaching head knowledge should be your goal as teacher. Creative variety in your teaching methods brings sparks to an otherwise dead class. This tool is as simple as asking, "What other ways can I use to teach this truth?" Find the answers, then implement. Your class will thank you for taking a creative risk. Creativity alone sparks interest. Interested pupils have a habit of coming back for more.

Tool Resource
Additional reading

100 Creative Teaching Techniques for Religious Teachers, by Phyllis Wezeman, will help spark your creativity.

31. Optimism (Free)

> *The point of living, and of being an optimist, is to be*
> *foolish enough to believe the best is yet to come.*
> — Peter Ustinov

Optimism is contagious. Classes never grow with a pessimistic teacher. Why would they? People drift toward positive vibes. What you give off each week in class either spurs members toward returning or diminishes their desire to make class attendance a habit. Optimism rejuvenates a dejected spirit. Our people have come after a week of working in a dog-eat-dog world. The last thing they need is pessimism from a teacher.

As you are optimistic about life, members catch the spirit. Collective optimism brings dividends to a lost world that is looking for answers. What greater optimistic message can we give than "Jesus wants to change our lives forever"? Be optimistic in your approach to life and the scriptures and reap the whirlwind of a happy, active, and vibrant class.

32. Courage (Free)
Times will come when classes need courage; courage by the teacher to resist members' attempts to minimize the need for outreach, and courage by class members not to abandon a class member during a time of crisis.

Satan never wants a thriving Sunday school class. He will do all he can to cause us to be fearful: fearful to do things differently, fearful to confront a lost community with the gospel. The more we give in, the more timid we become. We must be courageous, not in our own strength, but in the strength of our Lord.

Courage develops little by little. Teachers nurture this quality by encouraging members to step out of their comfort zones. These nonthreatening opportunities provide the footing to stand when courage is needed in a time of conflict or crisis.

33. Professionalism (Free)

Professionalism demonstrated week after week signifies to your class that what you do is important. Quality communications, whether in print, electronic media, or spoken word should portray professionalism. Mediocrity in the small things has a way of branding you a non-professional in the large things.

As a church musician, I have a coffee cup that says, "A joyful noise sounds better with practice." To paraphrase this in relation to Sunday school, "A Sunday school lesson sounds more professional with practice." If you are prone to stutter, stammer, and sprinkle your presentations with "uhs" and "and uhs," you may want to spend considerable time working on these issues that portray you as unlearned.

Let everything your class tries to achieve be of a professional quality. People tend to listen to our message more when we demonstrate skill and quality in our teaching.

34. Enthusiasm (Free)

Nothing great was ever achieved without enthusiasm.
— Author unknown

Your enthusiasm for your Lord and your Sunday school class, and your ability to communicate your passion is essential for your success.

Excitement is always in the air when a new church year begins and you have a new class. Then comes the later weeks when

44

the excitement wears off. Class members tend to get used to your voice. Without continued enthusiasm, you lose them. That doesn't have to happen.

Change your voice inflection. Boredom always comes with a monotone voice. Use variety. Change seating arrangements. Raise your eyebrows when you speak. Smile. Share what God is doing in your life. Share what God is doing in others' lives. Maintain your enthusiasm by maintaining your relationship with the Lord. Enthusiasm can't be faked or manufactured. Allow God to plant an unbounding love for your class in your heart.

A former parishioner, Charmen Dyer, always kept your attention. Her vibrant spirit and love for life impacted everyone she met. Even though you may have differed with her theologically, you never doubted that her faith influenced the way she lived. Enthusiasm for her Lord bubbled over into every realm of her life.

The enthusiasm class members see, they'll catch. More is caught than taught. Sunday school must resonate the message in the hearts of members that it is of utmost importance to their teacher and is worth being enthusiastic about.

35. Speed (Free)

Needs arise in Sunday school classes that need a quick response. Procrastination jolts many teachers when they've realized putting off preparation, delaying visiting a hurting member, or hesitating to register for a training event causes poor teaching, hurt feelings, and missed training opportunities. Speed becomes extremely important in certain situations.

Communications today have made it easy to stay in touch quickly. E-mail has put every class member at our fingertips. They can now instantly convey their needs, concerns, and prayer requests. The speed in which you respond can be a matter of life or death.

You can use speed to serve your class faster and better by:
• responding to requests in order of importance,
• immediately contacting a person in need upon hearing of the need,
• giving class members your e-mail address,

45

- responding to e-mail as soon as possible after it arrives,
- beginning lesson preparation on Monday for the next Sunday by dividing lesson preparation into small increments,
- in times of crisis, going quickly and personally,
- avoiding crowding your calendar, and
- registering early for all training events.

36. Agility (Free)

As with any organization, Sunday school ministry must maintain agility. Because it functions as a part of other church programs, pliability is required concerning special events, activities, revivals, and programs. If the church staff communicates effectively, you should never be caught by surprise. But surprises do happen. In those times, go with the flow. Support church leadership in the changes.

Other times, a crisis may occur among class members and their families. You may have to forgo a prepared lesson in order to meet the need of the moment. Such times are "once-in-a-lifetime" experiences to build relationships — relationship development that might never have happened over years of Sunday school lessons.

Agility is also desired in the area of your lesson plan. A lesson plan is only a guide. Never get so tied to your agenda that it becomes more important than those you teach. Classes need change. Sometimes you will recognize those changes midstream causing a readjustment to your original plans. Adapting to your new understanding will meet needs better than being rigid to a prior design.

37. Variety (Free)

You don't get harmony when everybody sings the same note.　　　　　　　　　　　　　　— Doug Floyd

Uniformity leads to boredom. Sameness week after week will dwindle any class down to nothing. If you have taught the same way, using identical methods and speaking in monotone, then variety is long overdue. Though we are creatures of habit, habitual teaching mannerisms can ruin an otherwise productive class.

Maybe you're not really creative. You don't have to be. Most Christian denominations have their own supplementary literature which contains teaching guidelines. Use the creative lesson plans in the material. Most are written by education ministry professionals.

Variety can be approached from many avenues: room setup, teaching methods, and creative outreach are just a few. As class members are kept guessing as to what the lesson will be like in the coming week, a sense of anticipation, intrigue, and interest develops.

As you focus on this chapter's thirteen tools, demonstrating each throughout the Sunday school, subtle differences begin to appear. Excitement, energy, and a "can do" spirit soon grows. The once mediocre, indifferent, and unfocused Sunday school structure is now becoming excellent, engaged, and centered on meeting needs of people.

---

1. George Barna, *The Habits Of Highly Effective Churches* (Ventura, California: Regal Books, 1999), p. 135.

Chapter 7

Tools That Provide Publicity

Christian leaders historically finish last when adopting the newest technology. Computers flourished long before they were finally placed in church offices. Yet, such reluctance abounds toward all attempts at using print, audio, video, and electronic media to promote the gospel. That must change if our Sunday schools are to reach the maximum number of people.

The following tools are meant to showcase ways to get the word out without a large expenditure of money and/or time. Some of these have never been used to promote Sunday school in most churches. Granted, you must be creative in using them, but they still can be employed effectively.

38. Newspaper (Free)
Most newspapers have religion editors or someone who handles religious news. They all print community news. If you are having a special guest for a high-attendance day, contact the religion editor and ask him to do a feature article. Better yet, write it yourself.

We once booked a Miss America pageant winner soon after she was crowned. The daily paper jumped at the chance of doing a front page feature article. The result: thousands of dollars of free publicity. Our church and Sunday school were packed that day.

Newspaper promotion among the 2003 BSSQ survey respondants garnered a 38 percent reporting of newspaper articles used to promote their church. What was surprising to me was that 52 percent of churches run newspaper ads. Newspapers are the promotion of choice for these churches with 80 percent use of articles and ads — well above any other media outlet.

Recently, an editor told me that the reason my articles seem to appear more than others is that I send him plenty of material to work with. Most church news items he receives are in the form of an announcement, small enough to fit in the calendar of events. Add more substance and you may find it as a news article and in the calendar of events. Add a quality photo and your chances are raised considerably in placing your news article.

All special days in Sunday school are potential opportunities to craft a newspaper article or feature. Tie it to a holiday, current event, or issue of national debate. Whatever the occasion, keep sending news items. Not all will be accepted, but many will.

39. News Releases (Free)

Closely related to newspaper articles and features is the news release. In fact, what you send the newspaper should be in the form of a news release. News releases also go to radio, television, and other media.

Your news release should state NEWS RELEASE in the top left hand corner. The right corner should state CONTACT, listing a contact person's name and telephone number.

Say your guest is doing a joint adult Sunday school assembly. Request that he send you a media kit. That kit will contain his news release. Adapt it to your situation, adding that he will be speaking at your church at a joint Sunday school assembly. Make mention that the public is cordially invited.

News releases promoting a Sunday school guest or event should be free of typos, printed on quality paper (professionally printed if possible), and give the basic who, what, when, why, and where.

40. Newsletter (Low Cost)

Most churches have one, but most churches print and mail poor quality newsletters. If what we do is substandard, we might be better off if we didn't publish one.

I hadn't realized how pitiful church newsletters had become until I saw one done with excellence. In fact, everything Jerry does conveys excellence. The print materials we put out rivals anything coming out of a professional printing press.

I do confess we have first-class printing equipment, but so do many churches who still print second-rate work.

After your office help receives adequate training, make sure every issue of your newsletter promotes Sunday school in some way. Be creative. Highlight a Sunday school teacher of the month. Focus on a class mission project. Report the number of contacts. Honor classes that are doing the work of Sunday school well. The church newsletter is the place to constantly stay in touch with Sunday school members and to encourage those who only attend church to unite with a class.

Tool Time

Advanced article series

Do a series of articles three weeks prior to a high-attendance day to prepare Sunday school leaders and members. For instance, for our September Encounters, a four-week attendance campaign, I used a series of three articles in our church newsletter during the month of August. They were titled: 1) Why have Church Encounter Sundays? 2) What will they involve? and 3) Why should you come?

41. Bulletin (Low Cost)

As with newsletters, bulletins should exemplify quality. Though limited in the amount of space for announcements, keep Sunday school events promoted.

The bulletin, in the absence of a church brochure, can be used on Sunday school visitation nights. By using the leftover Sunday bulletins you are being a good steward.

42. Radio (Free - Expensive)

As with newspapers, radio can publicize Sunday school events, activities, and high-attendance days. This medium is especially effective when a special guest is brought in.

Of respondents in the BSSQ survey, only 14 percent use radio spots. Added to the 24 percent who use community service announcements to radio, over a third promote their Sunday school and church in this way.

To avoid the cost of spots or ads, many of these churches understood that radio stations will run community service announcements for free. Combined with newspaper articles, posters, other print media, and television, radio coverage can be most effective.

Use radio coverage when you have an upcoming:
- well-known guest,
- high-attendance day,
- high-profile testimony, or
- Sunday school campaign

Thirty- or sixty-second spots or ads will cost you an average of between $6 and $10 each, depending on the market. Cut some of the expenses by making the spots or ads in-house but only if they can be produced with quality.

Tool Time

Keys to radio coverage
- Develop a relationship with radio dee-jays and/or owner.
- Try to tie your Sunday school promotion in a way that benefits you and the station.
- Send or personally deliver all news releases a week ahead of the event.
- Make it brief if used as community news.
- Produce a quality spot or ad.

43. Television (Free - Expensive)

Free television coverage is possible if you have a special guest coming who the general public would have an interest in hearing and seeing. If you schedule them to speak to a joint Sunday school assembly, that information can be reported at the beginning, during, or after the interview. Morning talk shows are always looking for guests.

According to the 2003 BSSQ survey, churches actually reported using more television spots as compared to radio spots (24 percent to 14 percent).

Expensive coverage occurs when you make a commercial or put on your own television program. Many churches air their services on cable television. If you do, use those opportunities to promote your Sunday school.

Tool Time
Scheduling an appearance
- Call and ask to speak to the program director. If they have an early morning show, also ask for that program director.
- Be brief.
- State who you represent, why you are calling, and why your guest would be worthy of an interview on their show.
- Promptly send any requested information on your guest.
- Try to secure a booking, but don't be pushy. Follow-up later if you sense they are not ready to make a commitment.

44. School/Civic Program Ads (Low Cost)
Promote your Sunday school event by taking out an ad in the high school football programs or any civic event being held in your city. Have someone in your church draw up a professional looking ad. These are particularly useful in publicizing youth Sunday school events.

Highlight the main features of your event. If a personality is involved, include his or her photo with the ad. Use your imagination. Be creative. The more eye catching the promo, the more people will notice.

As an evangelistic appeal, include a brief explanation of the gospel. The ABC's would do: accept, believe, and confess.

45. Thank-you Notes (Free - Low Cost)

Every action taken by individuals to support the Sunday school and Sunday school classes should be followed by a thank-you card. Thank-you cards express deserved appreciation. They also build relationships.

Class members enjoy hearing words of appreciation from their teacher. Written communication can have a greater impact than verbal. Members know we took the time to buy a card, write a note in our own words, and travel to the post office. Such effort does not go unnoticed.

Using your office equipment or personal computer, print some thank-you cards with your church or Sunday school class logo. If unable to print with a professional quality, pay to have some printed.

46. Business Cards (Low Cost)

Print business-sized cards for your Sunday school class or classes. Put the teacher's name, church, and class name on the front. Include contact information. Give cards to class members and ask them to give them out to friends and family.

A variation of this idea is to print up friend cards that say, "Because you are my friend, I want to invite you to our Sunday school class."

Use these cards at some point in a thirteen-week Sunday school emphasis, where you give class members thirteen cards and ask them to give out one a week inviting people to Sunday school.

47. Stationery (Low Cost)

Occasionally, letters will be sent to Sunday school class members, church family, and media to inform them of various events, activities, or announcements. Use your stationery to convey professionalism, warmth, and excellence.

Have stationery printed by a professional printer. Use top-quality paper if you can afford it. Individual classes can use church stationery or, if you want to be creative, you can design your own. Always include your church name with the class name. In addition, if class stationery is produced, always include the pastor and class teacher's names on the letterhead. Also, provide contact information.

48. E-mail (Free)

Electronic mail has now made it possible for Sunday school class members to stay in touch with each other easily and efficiently. What better way to access a prayer chain than through e-mail? Most people have personal computers and can provide an e-mail address.

In addition, e-mail access provides the means for the teacher to send supplementary material for the coming week's lesson as well as provide the lesson to class members who are bedridden at home.

Tool Time

E-mail helps
- Use e-mail only with each class member's permission and only for the uses they authorize.
- Avoid overuse.
- Do not share addresses. Make sure class members also understand they should keep addresses private.

49. Website (Free - Low Cost)

Consider setting up a Sunday school class website. Only do so with the consent of the church staff. If the church has a site, ask how your class or classes can give a strong Sunday school focus to the site.

Websites are great to have and can be used as an outreach tool. Make it professional. Promote the site through as many search engines as possible. Encourage class members to visit the site frequently.

Tool Time

Website considerations
- Enlist a knowledgeable computer whiz in your church (all churches have one)
- Consider having the following:
    Teacher focus
    Prayer requests
    Contact information

Coming Sunday school lesson
Calendar
Supplementary materials link
Chat area

One of the drawbacks of my 2003 BSSQ survey was my not including the Internet as a media promotion choice. While only 5 percent wrote that in under "other," this number is much higher. With the proliferation of church websites, this is fast becoming a tool of choice in promotion.

50. Word Of Mouth (Free)
The best method since the beginning of time to promote and publicize anything is still word of mouth. Class members who talk about what God is doing in their class will impact more people than any of the above media and publicity avenues. The key is creating such a moving spirit and love among class members that they will share it with others. We have the greatest subject: Jesus. The greatest gift: Jesus. And the greatest power source: Jesus.

In my 2003 BSSQ survey, 24 percent used word of mouth to promote their church and ministries. This number would probably be much higher since this percentage came from a write-in under "other media."

How do you motivate classes to spread the word? I have found that people will begin talking when:

1. *Class experiences touch them in a profound way.* Teach every week to impact class members. When God does a number on them, they'll let everyone know what's happening.

2. *They make the Great Commission a priority.* Until they "see the multitudes and have compassion on them," active mouths in telling others will be absent. Use every opportunity to stress Jesus' directive: "go and tell."

Other influences that cause word of mouth to catch fire include:
- spirit-filled teaching,
- prayer-saturated preparation,
- repeated life change in the classroom,
- encouragement and mentoring by the teacher, and
- God's timing.

These twelve publicity tools in this chapter, when used together, will simultaneously provide an overwhelming degree of information to the general public. Though some people still may not heed our invitation, they will note something is happening at the church and in the Sunday school class(es). Seeds planted through publicity will encourage people to "come and see." Hopefully, they will come and stay once they see why they should heed the invitation.

Chapter 8

Tools Involving Enrollment

Enrollment directly affects attendance. If you want more people to attend your class, begin to work on enrollment. Sunday school attendance will usually be a certain percentage of the enrollment. For most churches, that is around 40 to 50 percent. For churches doing a better job of ministering to members, that number can jump as high as 60 to 65 percent. Enrollment is only important to the degree it provides names and faces of people who should be in Sunday school.

I am amazed at how some Sunday schools are enamored with having 100 percent attendance. They would rather have a class with fifteen on the roll and fifteen present (which is highly unlikely on a continuing basis) than thirty on the roll and twenty present. Five more people would be in Sunday school than that with a smaller enrollment.

The following tools are given to help increase Sunday school enrollment for individual classes and/or the entire Sunday school ministry.

51. Enrollment Visitation (Free)

Schedule a night of church-wide visitation just for enrollment. Secure twenty visitation teams by asking members to help with this effort. Make individual visitation cards for people who are members of your church but don't belong to any Sunday school class.

Presently my church has over 125 people who are church members but do not belong to a class. In just a few weeks, we will be knocking on their doors and asking them to enroll in a class. The degree of our success will depend on the receptability of those we are visiting, how truly interested our visitors are in gaining new members, and prior experiences of those we visit with Sunday school.

Enrolling people in Sunday school/small group classes is important to our 2003 BSSQ respondents: 43 percent said their church considers enrolling people "extremely important"; 38 percent said "important"; 14 percent said "somewhat important"; while none replied "of no importance."

Yet, though a priority, effectiveness in enrollment is another matter. Responses showed that 47 percent said their efforts in enrolling people in Sunday school/small groups were "fair to poor"; 14 percent responded "excellent"; and 24 percent said "good."

James E. Harvey of Lifeway Christian Resources said, "I've collected a number of prospects who have visited my Sunday school class during the last six months. I discovered that nineteen of these people resided in the immediate community of the church. I decided I would sit down one Sunday afternoon and give these prospects a phone call, asking them if I could enroll them in Sunday school. I was surprised that I enrolled all nineteen of them! Not one said. 'No.' "[1] Many people are ready to join a class if we will ask them.

Tool Time

Enrollment do's & don'ts
* Do ask those who are being visited to fill out the enrollment card.
* Do visit in pairs, men with men and women with women.

- Don't coerce anyone to fill out an enrollment card.
- Do tell them, even if they do not enroll, you value their church membership and if they ever have a need to please call.
- Do ask the teacher or class leaders to follow-up soon after the enrollment.

52. Visitor Enrollment (Free)

A perfect time to enroll new members is the first time a person visits your class. Ask your class secretary to be on the lookout for new faces and to ask for that commitment. Let the visitor fill out the card.

Jane visited our class. She had never been involved with Sunday school before but appreciated our interest in her. That first Sunday she became a member. She later confessed after months of faithful attendance that the request for her to enroll was just the nudge she needed to become involved. She added that she probably would not have been back had we not made that inquiry.

53. Enrollment Goals (Free)

Enrollment goals set the bar for reaching people for Bible study through the Sunday school. Set at the beginning of the church year, goals become a measuring stick for how well we are doing.

Creative slogans for enrollment goals are helpful in bringing and keeping the emphasis on people's minds. For instance, "24 in 2004" or "204 in 2004" or "2,004 in 2004."

Simply setting a goal will not help you to reach the goal. You must plan specific actions that will provide the opportunity and incentive to enroll people in Sunday school. Set enrollment goals only if your Sunday school leadership is committed to reaching them.

54. Cold-call Enrollment (Free)

Technically, you can enroll people anywhere, any time, any place. Yet, most places our people find themselves are not conducive to cold calling. A church-wide visitation program to prospects is one possibility. Cold-call Enrollment is different from Enrollment Visitation, in that you are asking prospects you don't know to enroll. Enrollment Visitation targets church members who are not enrolled in a Sunday school class.

The more information one can give about their church, the more effective Cold-call Enrollment will be. At some point in the visit, the person(s) needs to ask if the host would mind you enrolling them in Sunday school. As in enrollment visitation, let the one you ask fill out an enrollment card.

55. Event Enrollment (Free)

Special church-wide events are unique opportunities to ask people to enroll in Sunday school. Such requests should be subtle in nature. A simple form at the bottom of the program asking if they would like to enroll in a Bible study class is appropriate.

Make sure the event where this request is made is one of quality. In an indirect way, the person will associate the quality of the event with the quality offered in a Sunday school class. A mediocre event is a turn-off to enrolling in Sunday school.

These tools equip classes in enlistment. Research proves that people in a class are more likely to become Christians than those who never unite with a class. The challenge is leading our people to be more conscious about how to add people to their roll instead of how to take some off. The old saying, "Out of sight, out of mind" applies here. We tend to forget about people when we never see their names. Names on our rolls are constant reminders to staff, teachers, and class leaders that each is a part of our family and needs our ministry.

---

1. Neil E. Jackson, *100 Great Growth Ideas* (Nashville, Tennessee: Broadman Press, 1990), p. 85.

Chapter 9

Unique Sunday School
Concept Tools

You cannot manipulate growth through the Sunday school. But, you can use some creative Sunday school concepts that on the surface are nothing new. Some church leaders find themselves using these ideas but do not realize it. A conscious awareness of a tool's benefit allows leaders to maximize its use.

Stacking builds commitment upon commitment. Room preparation builds room upon room. Commitment seekers build covenant upon covenant.

56. Stacking (Free)

Stacking builds commitment upon commitment. Stacking approaches building attendance group by group, program by program, and age group by age group. For instance, if you are seeking a high attendance on a certain Sunday, you build commitment into the program for the day. Children's Sunday school could have a large-group puppet show. Youth Sunday school could pump the teenagers with a high spirited Sunday school rally. Adult Sunday school possibly would begin with a joint Sunday school assembly in the sanctuary with a special guest testimony.

Further enhancement of this stacking of commitments is to combine all of your choirs for a special presentation in the worship service. Generally, when they commit to sing in worship, they also attend Sunday school.

Week in and week out, stacking is possible when classes are asked to set long term goals and develop a plan of action to reach them. The more classes you have to do this long-term planning, the more stacking takes place. For instance if you have 25 classes out of 30 that set long-term goals with specific plans to reach them, you have effectively stacked 25 classes. Allow them to set goals and write actions. All that you ask is that the goals be measurable, have a "God-like dimension" to reaching them, and be specific in the actions planned.

To assist classes with events they can tie to their outreach efforts, share any planned church-wide high-attendance days or Sunday school campaigns, special events, or special guest Sundays. Limit this goal setting to outreach only. Experience has taught me that when classes are asked to set goals and actions for outreach and ministry, ministry always wins out. Little outreach goal setting gets accomplished.

Tool Resource

Sample goal sheet

Class Name _____

Attendance: Our goal for (year) is to reach an average of _____ people in attendance by (end of church year).

Action 1: _____

Action 2: _____

Enrollment: Our goal for (year) is to reach an enrollment of _____ by (end of church year).

Action 1: _____

Action 2: _____

57. Room Preparation (Free)

The concept of room preparation seems to be a non-issue to most considering how few do it. Sunday school classrooms can create a warm, inviting spirit or a cold, unfriendly one. First remove any clutter. Second, prepare attractive bulletin boards that support the coming week's lessons or one that puts the spotlight on the lives of members. Whatever you do, do it well. Third, move chairs out of rows and into a half or whole circle. Remove any podium or stand.

The more you can make your classroom like your living room at home the better. Use live plants and home decorating items. Couches, throw pillows, and bean bags are an option for youth classes. Physical preparation of your room is only the beginning. Next, consider spiritual preparation.

Spiritual preparation is when you pray over the room before class members arrive. Imagine where each one usually sits. Pray over each member by name. Ask the Lord to bind Satan from your room, and for the Holy Spirit to work in the lives of members at your next meeting.

As members arrive, have some meditative Christian music playing, or if youth, lively contemporary Christian playing in the background. Greet members at the door with a smile on your face. Welcome each member with a handshake, a hug, or a pat on the back.

By doing all of the above, you will notice an immediate benefit. Class members will sense something special will happen that day and will be looking with anticipation as you open and expound God's Word.

Tool Time

Room busters
- Unclean and unkempt floors
- ABCs & 123s on the walls instead of Christian phrases, pictures, and similar items
- Poor heating and cooling
- Uncomfortable chairs
- Poor lighting

- Partition that blocks view of members when class is full
- Secular literature on shelves, floor, or in other areas
- Poor sound insulation to address sound levels from neighboring classes

58. Commitment Seekers (Free)

A unique tool to enlist lay people in promoting Sunday school events is what I call "Commitment Seekers." These people are best chosen from a pool of your best supporters. Whatever Sunday school event you want to reach the maximum number of people, ask these supporters to serve as "Commitment Seekers" — enlisting five or ten others who will commit to come to the event.

Demonstrate how to ask others for their commitment. End their request to come with a verbal and/or physical demonstration of that commitment. Depending on the kind of relationship between the commitment seeker and the person being invited, seal the commitment with a handshake, pat on the back, or a hug.

If you are wanting 100 people to come, ask twenty people to serve as "Commitment Seekers." If they invite and seal their commitment with ten others, 200 commitments will have been made. Being conservative with the math, if 50 percent of the commitments follow through, you will have your 100 in attendance.

Tool Time
Commitment Seeker enhancements
- Combine with other promotional efforts.
- Meet a need and choose something of interest. The more the event meets a need and is of interest, the more success "Commitment Seekers" will have in enlistment.
- The "Commitment Seeker" must first commit before he/she asks someone else to commit.
- Involve the pastor. When the pastor speaks, everyone listens.

These three concept tools will not impact Sunday school in and of themselves. Combined with other tools, they can contribute to reaching the maximum number of people; or, as in the case of room preparation, provide a proper environment for learning and retention.

Chapter 10

Tools Used
Before Sunday School

Teachers can have the best lesson prepared and the room can radiate with readiness; yet, what happens before Sunday school can bring all such well-laid plans to naught. If people come with feelings of unfriendliness, unable to find their way, and distracted by record keeping interruptions, Sunday school attendance and participation can be greatly hindered.

To prepare for the lesson and neglect what takes place before it begins is poor stewardship. Why go to the effort and not address such issues? Failing to do so dampens progress toward a vibrant Sunday school.

59. Greeters (Free)

A smiling faced person who greets arrivals makes one want to come to Sunday school. Sam Walton of Wal-Mart understood this concept and applied it to his chain. Warm, friendly greeters are at every entrance. Such a welcome gives an extra edge for his stores in making shopping a pleasant experience.

My 2003 BSSQ survey showed 86 percent of the churches said they had greeters. I question this number since I'm afraid many of these churches are considering their ushers as greeters who do no more than hand out bulletins. The survey did not make the distinction.

Real greeters at church not only give the impression of a warm and friendly Sunday school, they also assist with directions, needs, and parking issues as they arise. "They welcome people with a smile and a handshake. They are the ones who personally escort visitors to the appropriate rooms. They watch for people who appear lost or hunting for the right place. They look for the newcomers next week and greet them again."[1] The transition from parking lot to welcome center to classroom is made simpler, quicker, and more pleasant with greeters.

Some of our mega churches set the example in this area. Highland Park United Methodist Church in Dallas, Texas, uses "new-member" greeters and "all-church" greeters. New-member greeters seek all new members who join each Sunday, present new-member packets, and get them to reserved seating. "The team of sixty 'all-church' greeters," says Cathy Morgan, assimilation minister at HPUMC, "assists those getting off the buses, and generally helps those in need or with questions upon arriving at the church." Idlewild Baptist Church in Tampa uses a hospitality team that greets people upon arrival. Both churches employ a loving handshake, smile, and knowledgeable members to give direction, help, and hospitality.

All greeters should be trained. Enlist naturally outgoing personalities. Above all, secure volunteers who have a pleasant smile and who smile often. Normal church ushers who hand out bulletins but do nothing else should be avoided in your enlistment. Expressionless ushers who are uncomfortable speaking to others are a hindrance to reaping the benefits of greeters.

Tool Time
Greeter essentials
- Training — Only trained volunteers should serve as greeters
- Gender — Use a cross-section of male and female, young and old

68

- Location — Place at every entrance to your building and parking lot
- Enlistment tenure — Secure greeters for a year's service
- Sunday school proponent — They should love and be committed to the Sunday school

60. Welcome Center (Free)

A centrally located Welcome Center should be easily identified and known by all greeters. This is the first stop of visitors who come to your church. It should be attractive, well staffed, and ready for visitors at least thirty minutes before Sunday school. Place visitors' packets, layout of Sunday school class locations, and literature at the site.

Coffee, donuts, soft drinks, and orange juice are possible complimentary food items found at welcome centers. Use every means available to make visitors welcome. Wheelchairs, physical assistance, carrying Bibles, diaper bags, and non-walking children are simple gestures to help visitors settle in to your Sunday school.

I was somewhat perplexed that though the 2003 BSSQ survey respondents said greeters were in 86 percent of the churches, only 43 percent had a welcome center. This partly led me to consider that they were using their ushers as greeters. Most full-fledged greeter ministries have a welcome center.

Tool Resource

Greeter manual

The Ministry Of Church Ushers And Greeters, by Dr. Lindsay Terry, builds a greeter program that keeps visitors coming back to Sunday school.

61. Directional Signs (Minimum Cost)

Have you ever gone anywhere only to find that when you arrived, no directions were available for the specific location of your meeting? This tool tells visitors your church understands their needs. It is unreasonable to ask our guests to find their way. Well-placed directional signs give general directions to specific age group classes.

By grouping age groups together in certain buildings or parts of buildings, directional signs can be easily placed. Always include signs to restrooms, welcome center, church offices, and fellowship hall. Professionally produced and lettered signs, small but large enough to read, should be placed at strategic places outside the areas where people enter your facilities.

62. Records (Minimal Cost)

On the surface, record keeping would appear not to be much of a tool for building Sunday school. But poor record keeping is the best way to allow Sunday school members and prospects to fall through the cracks. The format is immaterial. Accuracy is key.

Accurate attendance must be kept if you are to measure your success or failure. In addition, correct enrollment figures help determine what outreach plans are necessary to reach more people.

Always enlist someone who sees record keeping as their ministry. Try to secure someone who has a mindset for outreach. Avoid signing up anyone for this position whose sole desire is to have 100 percent attendance. They will do whatever it takes — even taking people off the roll, if necessary.

Tool Time
Keys to effective record keeping
- Have a centralized Sunday school office.
- Have a Sunday school record keeper for each class and the entire Sunday school ministry.
- Remember the KISS acrostic (keep it simple, stupid).
- Complete records per class within the first fifteen minutes of class. Stress being on time to class members. Let them know they don't get counted after records have been turned in.
- Use computer-generated records. Office should print out a list of absentees per class to give to teachers and outreach leaders before the Sunday school hour is over.
- Avoid interrupting teaching time to answer record keeping questions.

Tool Resource

Church software

RDS Advantage for Windows is a very fast, flexible, and comprehensive computer software record keeping program.

Sunday school tools of greeters, welcome center, directional signs, and records create a positive experience for attendees when they arrive. When they enter the classroom, these positives tend to lead into others. Build on these and watch God honor your efforts.

---

1. Gary McIntosh, *The Exodus Principle* (Nashville, Tennessee: Broadman Holman, 1995), p. 155.

Chapter 11

Teacher Essential Tools

Building Sunday school is about building lives. When these lives face life's losses and disappointments, how will they stand? How will they deal with death, disease, and disaster? Daniel Webster offered helpful advice, saying, "If we work on marble, it will perish. If we work on brass, time will efface it. If we rear temples, they will crumble to dust. But if we work on men's immortal minds, if we imbue them with high principles, with just fear of God and love of their fellow-men, we engrave on those tablets something which time cannot efface, and which will brighten and brighten to all eternity."[1]

Such building is what teaching is all about. The following tools will equip Sunday school teachers to leave their marks on people's lives for all eternity.

63. Spiritual Gift Of Teaching (Free)

All teachers are not created equal. Many struggle week-after-week trying to teach something for which they are not gifted. Our

Sunday schools struggle because we have too many teachers who grapple with being effective, who hate their lack of accomplishments as teachers, and who, quite frankly, would rather be doing something else.

Such obvious poor enlistment is not from the lack of effort by enlistment committees. According to our 2003 BSSQ survey, 85 percent said their church makes every attempt possible to enlist Sunday school/small group leaders who have the spiritual gift of teaching. Thirty-three percent said they always do, while 52 percent said most of the time, and only 5 percent said never.

Secular education provides a wonderful illustration of teachers who missed their calling. My son's eighth grade teacher gave Allen a zero. Guess why? Biting his fingernails. Needless to say, I went to see this teacher. In the process of our conversation she said, "I don't like kids ... and I can't wait until I retire." She should have retired much sooner. In fact, she should have never been hired.

Spiritually gifted teachers possess certain characteristics that set them apart. Let's look at Philip and the Ethiopian treasurer. Gifted teachers always:

1. *Draw near* — "Then the spirit said unto Philip, 'go near, and join thyself to this chariot' " (Acts 8:29). Gifted teachers will go to great lengths to get close to their students.

2. *Want understanding* — "And Philip ... said, 'Understandest thou what thou readest?' " (Acts 8:30). Asking for understanding implied more than a willingness to share knowledge. It portrayed a deeper realization of helping the eunuch truly grasp the meaning.

3. *Preach/teach Jesus* — "Then Peter opened his mouth, and began at the same scripture, and preached unto him Jesus" (Acts 8:35). Spiritually gifted teachers point others to the Master teacher. Fine oratory is nothing more than fine oratory, not spirit-filled, spirited teaching.

Across our land the debate rages about the many and varied understandings of spiritual gifts. "Observations of growing churches reveal it is not the different understandings of spiritual gifts that cause a church to grow or decline, but it is the use or lack of use of spiritual gifts that make the difference."[2]

Tool Resource
Finding your spiritual gift

Your Spiritual Gift Can Help Your Church Grow, by Peter Wagner, is an excellent reading source on spiritual gifts.

64. Love Of Age Group (Free)

All teachers love their pupils, right? No! Not even church teachers. With words we say we do; but in actual practice, we give ourselves away. Take the secular teacher mentioned in the previous tool. She did not even like children, let alone love them.

Spiritually gifted teachers have an unbridled compassion for those they teach. A clear indication not to accept an offered teaching position is when you don't particularly care for the age group.

Nurturing this tool comes with nurturing your relationship to Christ. The more you grow in love for him, the more you will love others.

From a practical standpoint, this tool can be used when we speak to our students, face crises together, and spend quality and quantity time outside the classroom. Love means unwavering devotion to class members throughout their lifetimes, during times of joy and sadness.

65. Flexibility (Free)

"Years ago, Frank Lloyd Wright was given the impossible task of building the Imperial Hotel in Tokyo. No comparable construction job ever before had been undertaken. With patience he laid plans for the immense building in this land of earthquakes and terrible tremors. After carefully reviewing the situation, he found that eight feet below the surface of the ground lay a sixty-foot bed of soft mud. Why not float the great structure on this and in some way make it absorb the shock of an earthquake? After four years of work, amid ridicule and jeers of skeptical onlookers, this most difficult building in the world was completed, and soon arrived the day which tested it completely. The worst earthquake in 52 years caused houses and buildings all around to tumble and fall in ruins. But the Imperial Hotel stood, because it was able to adjust itself to the tremors of the earth."[3]

Teachers cannot remain rigid and firm when tremors come. Working with volunteers requires teachers to be flexible. Teachers must go with the flow when sick children take out parents, when the air conditioning for their classroom goes out on Saturday night, and when the pastor announces an unexpected schedule change.

Such interruptions can be an instrument for teachers to live out their faith in front of pupils. To become stressed, upset, and irritated is to give the impression their faith is shallow, to say the least. Similar times are excellent opportunities to teach their class compassion, patience, and understanding. Teachers can stand tall when they are able to adjust to the tremors that come from everyday life.

66. Support (Free)

No teachers can effectively build their class without support — support from church staff and class members. Support comes with trust. Trust must be earned. I'm convinced the most powerful Sunday school class is the one whose class members trust and completely support their teacher. The only nullification of their impact is when they lose pastoral support.

Mr. Johnson had such a class. He had ministered so effectively to its members they considered him their pastor. That's where the rub came. Because class members were so critical of their pastor, it soon carried over into the relationship between Mr. Johnson and the pastor. Needless to say, after the pastor chose to keep this class out of the loop, the effectiveness of the class in the community was limited.

This tool is manifested through prayer, guidance, encouragement, and assistance. When the teacher, staff, and class members work in triune — walking in stride, side by side — watch out world! The potential for community change — life change — is firmly within reach.

67. Leadership (Free)

Sunday school classes either survive or thrive ... and they do it based on the quality of leadership. Every class needs a dynamic Christian leader to follow. Most of the time that person is the Sunday school teacher, but not always. Whoever the person may be, he or she must set the example in personal devotion, outreach, and ministry. A class will emulate the perceived class leader. Spiritual leadership reaps spiritual results. Worldly or lukewarm leadership brings about worldly results.

How can this leadership tool be put to use? First, only place in the role of Sunday school teacher those individuals who consistently demonstrate godliness and the spiritual gift of teaching. Second, before you give sanction to their teaching, ask that they commit to a personal quiet time and participation and support for outreach. Third, stress life-change teaching over transferring head knowledge. Fourth, ask for unwavering commitment to preparation. "You can't look at a passage on Saturday night and teach well Sunday."[4]

Sometimes leadership development takes time. It may mean your taking one teacher at a time and modeling before them leadership qualities that you want demonstrated in front of class members.

Tool Resource

Leadership skill journal

Build a personal leadership skill journal. As you and your leaders read books of successful leaders and watch their tapes, jot down ways they led by example, communicated, propagated their vision, and rallied people to service. Commit to practice, implementing one skill a week. Evaluate your progress at week's end.

The Scale — Using a scale of 1-10, chart your progress.

Communication	_____
Example	_____
Response from people	_____

Realistically, mark your starting point. Seek to move up one number on the scale each week.

68. Knowledge (Free)

Gaining knowledge in teaching skills remains a challenge for all church leadership. Make every attempt to constantly further your knowledge as teacher or as a leader of teachers. We have more resources available to us today than ever in the history of our nation. Most of us take it for granted. Yet, teaching skills must be constantly sharpened. It is easy to get in a rut. Knowledge of new teaching methods, outreach programs, and ways of conducting Sunday school keeps us on the cutting edge of ministry.

If you have taught the same way for fifty years, I can almost guarantee you have become an ineffective teacher. The gospel never changes, but our methods must. Bill is a case in point. Bill loves the lecture method. In fact, that's all he does in his class. No questions, no discussion, and no involvement. Needless to say, Bill's class has steadily declined over the years.

Notice that this tool is about gaining knowledge of teaching and outreach methods. Don't confuse this with teaching head knowledge. Knowledge of new and improved teaching/outreach methods is an essential tool. Teaching head knowledge in the classroom must be changed so that the knowledge taught brings about life change.

These teacher essential tools can transform teachers into dynamic instruments of God. Their effectiveness will be seen as class members begin to take on the likeness of Christ. Your implementation of these tools will immediately impact classes for years to come.

---

1. Daniel Webster, Morning Glory, July 3, 1993. Internet online. Available from <www.bible.org/illus.asp?topic_id=1091>[July 3, 1993].

2. Gary McIntosh, *Biblical Church Growth* (Grand Rapids, Michigan: Baker Publishing Group, 2003), p. 116.

3. A. Smith, in Resources, #2. Internet online. Available from <www.bible.org/illus.asp?topic_id=564>.

4. Josh Hunt, *You Can Double Your Class in Two Years or Less* (Loveland, Colorado: Group Publishing, 1997), p. 39.

Chapter 12

Facility Tools

"Before you invite guests over, first clean the house."[1]
— Lee Strobel

Vivid images of a church I served part-time while going to college come to mind when I consider facility tools. This church, though filled with some wonderful people, had allowed their facilities to get in deplorable condition. The sanctuary had at one time been sprayed for termites but the baseboards were never replaced. Every foot or so along the wall were holes that had been drilled into the wall and were left that way. Classrooms were untidy, bathrooms stained, old, and unpleasant. It was no surprise to me why people visited only once.

This was a no-brainer for our 2003 BSSQ survey churches; 91 percent said the way their church views the way they keep their facilities is "very important" or "important."

They understand facilities make lasting first impressions. Sunday school classes are impacted positively when we have clean rooms, adequate space, and necessary comforts.

69. Clean Facilities (Low Cost)

People who visit our churches notice if they are clean. They don't live in homes that are dirty and they don't want to go to a dirty church either. "How we decorate and present our facilities tells people a lot about our church and our values."[2] Every church, no matter how plain the outside structure, can maintain a clean facility that leaves positive impressions on visitors.

Where cleanliness is so crucial is in two areas: restrooms and the preschool/children's area. Statistics prove that restrooms are an important concern for visitors. If you want to remodel, do your restrooms first. The reason we avoid certain gas stations on the highway is the same reason we turn people off who come to our church: unclean and unkempt restrooms.

My pastor recognized this need before I did. Our restrooms were clean but they were old and run down. I had no idea how much he was willing to spend to bring them up to standard. Would you believe we spent $8,000 per restroom? The cost was worth it.

Your church may not have money to spend on updating restrooms. But every church can keep what they have clean.

70. Space (Free - Expensive)

Johnny came one Sunday morning, poked his head in the door, saw that the class was full, and immediately left. People will not continue to come to a Sunday school class that is more than 80 percent full.

A full classroom is deceptive. It can lead the class and teacher to think they are doing a wonderful job when in fact they are not. If the class is full with 40 percent present, it is easy to forget about the 60 percent absent. Such a class needs a larger room or another class needs to be started.

How do you determine if you have adequate space? "In a class-room, take the total square footage (minus clutter, pianos, cabinets, and so on) and divide it by the space requirements needed for the learners (early childhood) — 30 to 35 square feet per pupil; children (grades 1-6) — 25 to 30 square feet per pupil; youth (grades 7-12) — 20 to 25 square feet per pupil; and adults — 0 to 20 square feet per pupil."[3]

Tool Time

Space savers
- Offer to split into two Sunday schools.
- Remove anything that takes up space that is not essential to the room or teaching.
- Move to a larger room.
- Start a new class.
- Move some classes to a home setting.

71. Creature Comforts (Expensive)

Unfortunately, we live in a day where creature comforts have spoiled us. We can argue that people will go watch a ball game during inclement weather so they should not mind that our classrooms are less than comfortable. Wrong! People will not continually come to Sunday school if the classroom is too hot or too cold. Our bodies have become used to air conditioning and heating systems and it is foolish to think otherwise.

Even metal chairs have become a problem as more and more churches have gone to padded chairs. Yet, truth rests with our desire for comfort. If people are genuinely comfortable, they are more likely to listen and participate in the Sunday school lesson.

Supplying creature comforts is expensive. They are a necessity in meeting the needs of our members.

Tool Time

Easing creature comfort cost
- Do an energy audit.
- Change the type of energy you use, based upon the results of the energy audit, if necessary.
- Add more insulation.
- Set your thermostats and put a lock on them so church members cannot constantly change the readings.
- Schedule all extra meetings in one central building or meeting room, if possible. Heat and cool only that room.

Making use of these facility tools will not in themselves bring about growth. But their absence will indeed hinder growth. We would be wise to see that our church/classrooms are clean, space is adequate, and creature comforts are provided.

---

1. Lee Strobel, *Inside the Mind of Unchurched Harry and Mary* (Grand Rapids, Michigan: Zondervan, 1993), p. 196.

2. Gary McIntosh, *The Exodus Principle* (Nashville, Tennessee: Broadman Holman, 1995), p. 89.

3. John R. Cionca, *Solving Church Education's Ten Toughest Problems* (Wheaton, Illinois: Victor Books, 1994), p. 106.

Chapter 13

Tools That Are
Sunday School Campaigns

I will always remember the thrill of hearing the applause break out at my first full-time church when the Sunday school high attendance goals were announced — and we had reached them. That first feeling of experiencing the joys of realized expectations has led me to see the extreme value in having Sunday school campaigns.

Sunday school campaigns and high attendance days are a part of our 2003 BSSQ survey respondent calendar: 33 percent have yearly events; another 33 have campaigns three times a year; and still another 14 percent have them two times a year.

In and of themselves, Sunday school campaigns will not bring about long-term growth, but they can give a Sunday school a shot in the arm by a higher attendance for a Sunday or group of Sundays, encourage church staff, and provide a new list of potential prospects.

The Sunday school campaigns can come in the form of a four-week emphasis, high-attendance days, and a thirteen-week summer drive.

72. Four-Week Emphasis (Low Cost)

When you choose to have a four-week Sunday school emphasis, you:
- build attendance from Sunday to Sunday,
- involve more age groups,
- build momentum, and
- impact an entire month, not just a week.

A four-week emphasis uses a multiplicity of tools. The more tools you use during this emphasis, the more likely you will reach all of your goals.

The pastor is the key to the success of any four-week Sunday school emphasis. He must be vocal, encouraging, and out front promoting the four weeks. A staff member can do all of the planning and implementation, but the pastor must lead. Without his leadership, the church membership will not see the campaign as important ... and will not come on board in reaching church-wide goals.

Media advertising is also an important element in a four-week campaign. Though cost is a factor, much can be done in the way of in-house posters, flyers, and other promotions. News releases sent as community service announcements should be sent to every newspaper and radio station in the area.

Tool Resource
Sample four-week campaign
September Encounters
September 8 — Adult Encounter
- Special joint adult assembly with Michael McCain, Christian dramatist
September 15 — Youth Encounter
- Joint youth Sunday school rally with Billy Kennedy, basketball coach from Southeastern University

84

September 22 — Children's Encounter
- Children's "Pick And Choose Fun Fest" after the morning service

September 29 — Church Encounter
- Combined choirs in the morning service
- Special children's feature in a joint children's Sunday school assembly

73. High Attendance Days (Low Cost)

High attendance days are special Sundays that make for a unique time to reach the maximum number of people in Bible study. Resurrection Sunday (Easter Sunday), the Sunday before Valentine's Day, and the first Sunday beginning a new church year are ideal times to have a high attendance day.

Enhance this day with a series of articles in your newsletter prior to the event, promoting various aspects of the day. Use your bulletin, pulpit, and church letter to promote it. Again, involve your pastor in every aspect of the promotion. A personal letter from him to every church member goes a long way in encouraging attendance.

As in Sunday school campaigns, high attendance days are readily used by churches (2003 BSSQ survey) — 90 percent of the churches have them at least once a year and only 10 percent never have a high attendance day.

Individual classes can assist in reaching a maximum number of people by setting a class goal, contacting all members and absentees and inviting everyone on their prospect list. The more people involved in the promotion and implementation, the greater potential for turnout on that day.

Make use of the unique Sunday school concepts of stacking and commitment seekers mentioned in chapter 9.

Tool Resource
Sample high attendance day
Heart-to-Heart Sunday — February 9
- Telephone Blitz on Saturday, February 8
- Worship service built on the subject of love

85

- Special guest in a joint adult assembly at 9:15 a.m. in the sanctuary
- Children's Valentine Party after the 10:30 service
- Heart Exchange — in the morning services, everyone will receive a paper heart and pin during Sunday school and before worship. At a point in the service, each person will go and pin their heart on someone who has touched his/her life spiritually.

74. Thirteen-Week Summer Emphasis (Low Cost)

Longer emphasis events require leaders to continually keep the emphasis before the people. Enthusiasm can wane, but that can be avoided with enhancements by the church staff. A thirteen-week emphasis needs to include three high attendance days: one at the beginning, middle, and end. Give the emphasis a name. Try to come up with a name that fits the season of the year, purpose of the campaign, or something that ties into your church mission statement.

A possible way to enhance this campaign is to ask people to commit to eleven of thirteen weeks. Print up commitment cards. Ask teachers to display the cards in their classes. Print up business-sized cards that say, "Because you are special to me, I want to invite you to (name of your church)." Give everyone thirteen cards and ask them to give one out each week.

Tool Resource
Involving Sunday school teachers

Try this: at your next teachers and officers' meeting, divide the group into four teams with teachers from each age group on each team. Ask them, over the next month, to design a Sunday school campaign. Ask only that:
- it involves all age groups,
- it reaches out to the community,
- it includes a high attendance goal, and
- it includes a promotion plan.

Once completed, ask someone to prepare a printed copy. Share with the teachers and officers that you will try to use their teams' plans over the coming year. Then do your best to use one or more of the plans.

Tool Resource

Successful campaign features

Consider these aspects when developing Sunday school campaigns:

- **Detailed Plan** — Every aspect of your campaign must be outlined in intricate detail. One oversight can wreak havoc.
- **Maximized Involvement** — The more people involved in implementing the plan, the greater the ownership. Once owned, people will do what it takes to bring success.
- **Telephone Blitz** — Experts tell us we can increase our attendance by 20 percent on any given Sunday simply by calling our members. It would behoove us to call.
- **Varied Publicity** — Use every conceivable means to publicize your campaign. Most are free. All are effective.
- **Pastoral Leadership** — The pastor must be highly visible in promoting the campaign. Without his prominence, no attendance drive will succeed.
- **Conflict Avoidance** — Some months are better than others in having campaigns. Avoid months with major holidays or school breaks.
- **Scriptural Tie-ins** — If possible, tie your theme to scripture. Friend Days, Resurrection Sunday, and Heart-to-Heart Sundays all link well to scripture.
- **Wow Factor** — Do something or bring in a guest that you know will leave the congregation spellbound. The more "wow moments" you can have, the greater return on your efforts.

Sunday school campaigns can truly impact your Sunday school. Use your imagination to come up with creative themes. Cover every detail. Promote with every publicity tool available. When you do, watch and see how God will indeed honor your efforts.

*Sunday school campaigns give a boost to the body of
Christ as adrenaline does to the physical body.*

Chapter 14

Network Tools

In a day of individualism, many churches are throwing away ties to their denominations, not so much in affiliation, but in actual use of their resources. Much is available throughout our conventions to assist us — to network in doing Sunday school together. Particularly if we are new to the ministry or are lay persons with limited knowledge of Sunday school work, our state, district, parish, association, or presbytery can be of great assistance.

When I asked our 2003 BSSQ survey churches if they networked with their local, state, and national offices for help in training and resources, 58 percent said often or sometimes, 10 percent said seldom, and 14 percent said never. Other responses were not applicable since they came from independent churches.

Our state Sunday school leadership, directors of missions, district director, parish minister, and the associational, district, or parish Sunday school directors are each networking avenues that have leadership, resources, and a willingness to help us when needed.

75. State Sunday School Leadership (Free - Low Cost)

Training Sunday school workers presents a challenge for church leadership. Most of us, though capable of leading such training, don't have the time to put together the creative training visuals and materials. State Sunday school workers have this material on hand. Most states see that their leaders are trained in the latest teaching methods. They also furnish many of the visuals and handouts needed to make a training event meaningful.

Churches can enlist state workers to come lead a conference, many times at no cost to the church. Also, these workers can be reached by phone to answer any of your needs related to Sunday school.

Tool Time

Rules of engagement
- Call early. State workers are in demand. Calling early assures you of getting a date you want.
- Go in with other churches in the area. If cost is involved, they can share the cost.
- Ask for the state's best workers. You may or may not get them, but at least they will know what your desires are and can give you the best that is available. These may be people in your area that the state gives as an alternative for those in their office.
- Follow through on any agreements on your part. A positive dealing with the state will lead to beneficial networking in the future.

76. Director Of Missions, District Director, Or Parish Minister (Free)

Key help is always available to us through our director of missions (SBC), district director (UMC), or parish minister (PUSA). This person is the most accessible, as well as the most interested in helping our Sunday schools grow. The director of missions, district director, or parish minister is usually knowledgeable in the Sunday school area, many having pastored churches in their former roles. If they don't have an answer to your need, they can get you to the right person.

When talking with a director of missions, district director, or parish minister, be specific about your need. Share only what is necessary for them to know what you want. Be courteous of their time. Thank them for their help. Offer to be of assistance to them when needed. Give help when they request it.

77. Associational, District, Or Parish Sunday School Directors (Low Cost)

Though less trained than state office workers, associational, district, or parish Sunday school directors accepted their positions because they wanted to serve. They are a valuable help in answering basic Sunday school questions. They, too, can be enlisted to lead Sunday school training events. Because they live in your area and get far fewer requests for help, they are usually readily available.

If your church will be using associational, district, or parish workers, a common courtesy is to pay their travel expenses and a small honorarium. Some state offices will assist with this cost.

Tool Time

Considerations
• Associational, district, or parish workers are usually lay people with limited training.
• Try to attend a conference they lead before you enlist their help.
• Weigh the benefits of their leading compared to the sacrifice you are asking of your workers to attend. If you are not sure a conference led by associational, district, or parish Sunday school workers will be an above average experience, don't use these workers.

We are all in Sunday school work together. We need each other. Remember: The more knowledge, the more help, the more support you have doing Sunday school work, the greater your chances in building a growing Sunday school class and/or ministry.

Chapter 15

Prospect Discovery Tools

With the proliferation of churches in our communities, people have more choices than ever as to which church they will attend. Many will not attend yours until they see a church that cares. First contact is the means to show we care. Finding these people, these prospects, is not always an easy task. But once we do, and we visit in the home, at least one visit from them will be the outcome.

The vast majority of the BSSQ survey churches (72 percent) said they had a system in place for discovering prospects. This is indeed encouraging because that is the number one need if you are going to have an ongoing Sunday school outreach ministry.

Finding prospects and cultivating them is hard work, but necessary. We can find prospects by doing door-to-door canvassing and telephone surveying. Additional names can be secured from utility turn-ons and through scouring school annuals.

78. Door-to-Door Canvassing (Free)
Going door-to-door to do a people search provides a great way to gather prospect names for your church. Mapping off your church

with a five-mile radius and then breaking that down into sections, you can survey your church surroundings little by little, one street at a time.

The benefit of this survey is that you make face-to-face connections with people who live near your church. Most will be willing to take part in a religious survey. The hoopla over telemarketing has come because of people selling something or asking for money. Neither of these are a part of door-to-door canvassing.

Tool Time
Safety considerations
- Teenagers make great surveyors. If you send teens, make sure an adult is with them. They don't have to go to the door, but the adults should remain at the street within sight.
- Men survey with men, ladies with ladies.
- If a woman answers the door, men should complete the survey outside, while standing at the door.
- If you are invited inside, go, but only if you are invited. Stay only as long as it takes to complete the survey. Any reluctance on the surveyor's part to go in should be taken as a sign to remain outside.
- If a man answers the door, women surveyors should remain outside and complete the survey at the door.
- Never send anyone to do survey work by themselves.

79. Telephone Survey (Free)
One of the simplest ways to secure prospect names is by conducting a religious telephone survey. Using church members as calling teams (ten to a team; four teams), forty families a week and 160 a month can be surveyed. Of that number you can count on from one to two families being prospects for every ten called.

Because of the demanding nature of these calls, it is best to enlist callers for a three month period. The survey should include basic information: name and telephone number (obtained from telephone book), correct address, questions on whether they attend church/Sunday school (weekly, monthly, seldom, or never), if they are a church member (where?), if they are Christians, and if we can we enroll them in Bible study. Give out packets on Sunday to be returned by the next Sunday.

Tool Resource

Telephone survey suggestions
- Avoid early and late times to call (before 8 a.m. and after 9 p.m.).
- Identify yourself: name and church.
- Stay focused on survey. Answer any questions. If you don't know the answer, tell them you don't know, but that you will find out. Once you get the answer, relay the information.
- If they refuse to do the survey, say you are sorry for having bothered them, thank them for their time, and hang up.

80. New Connects (Free)

In some parts of the country you can no longer secure new connects (utility turn-ons) because of privacy issues. Other places you can. This tool is valuable because these people have just recently moved into the home. Some will have moved from across town, but most will be new people in your community.

These are ready prospects. The quicker you can get into these homes, the better. To leave an even better impression, take a plate of freshly baked cookies, a welcome packet, or both.

81. School Annuals (Free)

Names of every child in your community can be found in the school annual. Secure a copy and print a list of the names, leaving room for parent's name, address, and phone number. Circulate the list among parents who have children that age. Ask them to list as much information as they know on each name. If you have any mail carriers in your church, these are excellent people to help with identifying parent names.

After the list has made it around to parents, let the children help with securing information. Once this list has been completed, make a prospect card for each name that has completed information. Make contact with these families to determine their prospect status.

Some tools regarding prospect discovery begin as a ministry project. The next six tools can be described as such:

82. Literacy Classes (Low Cost)

"The appalling fact in the richest nation of the world (USA), ten million adults are almost totally illiterate in the English language."[1] With such a need, what a wonderful way to provide ministry. In the process, you secure prospects for your church.

Make sure that your motivation is to meet the needs of the illiterate while providing an opportunity to share Christ. A by-product is a ready prospect list, but this should not be our motivation.

Most of our churches have retired English teachers. Enlist one of these to teach the class. Make sure you provide the best possible literacy training. Don't even attempt such a class until you are satisfied it will be done with excellence. The cost involved will be for leadership materials, though some can be found free, as listed below. Pupils can purchase what they need, or if they can't, the church should provide for them.

Tool Resource

Teaching manual

The Adult Education Basic Education Teacher's Toolkit is downloadable from <www-tcall.tamu.edu>.

83. Marriage Enrichment Weekends (Low Cost)

Strengthening home and family continues as a major need across our land. Marriage Enrichment Weekend is the perfect tool to meet a need and touch families for your church in the process.

Choose a centralized location to have this weekend experience. The local library, civic building, or similar setting that is away from the church is more conducive to attracting non-church attendees.

Promote the event heavily in your community beginning a month prior to starting the class. A great resource for this class is *The Five Love Languages* by Dr. Gary Chapman. The text is easily adaptable to a weekend conference.

At the end of the weekend, say, "Because it is impossible for us to cover everything that will enrich our marriages in one weekend, let me invite you to a Sunday night class at our church, beginning next Sunday at 5 p.m., that will allow us to continue our time together."

Between the time when the Marriage Enrichment Weekend ends and the new class begins, send a personal invitation to come to the class either through the mail, or if time is a factor, over the phone.

The new class roll brings fresh names to add to your church prospect roll.

84. Divorce Recovery Workshops (Low Cost)

The National Center for health statistics recently released a report which found that 43 percent of first marriages end in separation or divorce within fifteen years. Many of these people never recover and are prone to repeat the process in a second or third marriage.

A Divorce Recovery Workshop is designed to help divorcees know how to deal redemptively with their divorces and move on with their lives.

As with the Marriage Enrichment Weekend, host the Divorce Recovery Workshop in a centralized location away from your church facility. If you feel a real need to continue with a support group at the end of the workshop, invite the attendees to a new support group at your church.

Again, put on a first-class workshop. Choose your best facilitator and promote well.

Tool Resource

Divorce recovery

The Fresh Start Divorce Recovery Workbook, by Bob Burns and Tom Whitman, is a great supplemental resource.

85. Mother's Day Out (Expensive)

This tool provides ready prospects through providing loving and quality care for preschoolers in a safe, clean, and appropriate facility. The atmosphere created by stimulating activities, learning experiences, toys, and equipment gives children room to have lots of fun as they grow and develop. Mother's Day Out is generally shorter in duration than a full weekday education program.

Mother's Day Out should be used if it is seen as an outreach tool. The wear and tear on your building, plus the drain on human resources, can outweigh any benefits without such an outward focus.

Safety for the children and screening of workers must also be considered when starting a Mother's Day Out program.

All names of families who register their children in Mother's Day Out should be given to the pastor or education minister to be used as potential church prospects.

86. Weekday Early Education (Expensive)

Moving beyond what Mother's Day Out offers, a full Weekday Early Education program provides a complete educational day for preschoolers. The same concerns and purpose for Mother's Day Out is true for Weekday Early Education. I admit my concerns for both of these ministries for preschoolers is based on negative experiences I've seen with each in different churches.

As with any ministry in the church, if it is not a part of fulfilling the Great Commission, we need not go there. Both of these ministries are great avenues to meet needs of preschoolers and provide a continuing list of prospects to be reached with the gospel.

Tool Resource
Preschool education reading
Wee (Weekday Early Education) Administrative Guide, by Bob Couch and Lois Gamble, is usable for both Mother's Day Out and Weekday Early Education.

87. Sports Teams
Nothing generates more interest and enthusiasm than church sports teams. Used as an outreach tool, they can reach the lost more than any single evangelism tool. Two criteria should be stressed to each team: 1) The team must be composed of half its

members who are Christian and half who are non-Christian, and 2) In order to play, you must be willing to listen to a gospel presentation at the end of every game.

With non-Christians on the team, you can expect some non-Christian outbursts and behavior. Most, though, will respect the prevailing Christian atmosphere and act accordingly.

All team rosters become ready prospect files. As you follow through in homes, you will be amazed at how many you will reach.

Tool Resource

Coaching guide

A Youth Basketball Coaching Guide, by Danford Chamness, helps you build a team.

These avenues for obtaining prospects can meet real needs, as well as give your outreach efforts a boost in potential prospects. As you meet real needs, reaching participants will be made easier as hearts will be made tender through intentional ministry.

---

1. Thomas G. Sticht, 2001 International Reading Association, Inc., Gale Group, Oct.-Nov. 2001.

Chapter 16

Tools For Teacher Training

"In the study of ninety top leaders from a variety of fields, leadership experts Warren Bennis and Burt Namus made a discovery about the relationship between growth and leadership: 'It is the capacity to develop and improve their skills that distinguishes leaders from followers.' "[1] Sunday school teachers by nature of their position are placed in leadership roles. Training is not an option. Before any teacher accepts a position, he/she needs to understand they are expected to attend training opportunities as they arise or complete some self-study.

Related to offering training for Sunday school teachers, 43 percent offer training yearly; 19 percent quarterly; and 10 percent weekly. Only 14 percent never offer teacher training.

These churches, overall, understand that going on the "overflow" only lasts so long. Eventually, all that teachers know, all that they have mastered, spills out *ad nauseam*. Teaching becomes routine. They wallow in a spiritual wasteland where decay sets in. An imperceptible harm pervades their thinking when they subconsciously decide to forgo trying anything new. Motivation dies. Receiving ongoing training rekindles that motivation.

Ralph Waldo Emerson said, "Unless you try to do something beyond what you've already mastered, you will never grow." Consistent growth kindles motivation. Facilitate your personal growth and training by:

- building in accountability. Being responsible to someone else motivates you to achieve what's being asked.
- reaching for the impossible. You will be amazed at how people rise to your level of expectation.
- praying. God's power source magnifies our attempts at growth.
- goal-setting. Measurable goals become a tool to track progress and encourage ongoing efforts.
- modeling. Find another teacher who models what's being taught.

The following tools are only meant to whet your appetite for further training opportunities. Use your creativity and come up with many variations of the two general tools.

88. Group Training (Low Cost)

Possibilities abound for teachers to participate in group training. Each denomination offers training events at the national, state, district, association, presbytery, and church levels. Generally, the higher you go up the ladder toward national training gatherings, the caliber of leadership rises.

Greater benefits from group training come when you prepare yourself ahead of time.

- Secure resources if possible — reading the text before the conference. If the facilitator is an author and is training on the subject matter of his or her book, secure a copy of the book.
- Come early. Sit up front. Fewer distractions happen when you are near the facilitator.
- Take notes. We remember more when we write it down.
- Notice who answers or asks questions. If you are asked to make small groups, get in a group with these people. They are probably those from whom you can learn because of their inquisitive nature.

- Come with an open mind and a willingness to question past ways of teaching.
- If the facilitator will be staying for lunch, ask if you may eat with him/her or meet for a brief discussion at a later time. Use it as an opportunity for further feedback on any questions you may still have.
- Read over your notes once returning to your room after each session.
- Decide on three to five actions you will implement upon returning to your church.

Tool Resource
Which training? — decision time

Pick four conferences that would be of interest to you. Choose a national, state, district/association/parish, and church conference.

Use the following checklist to help you decide: National = 4, State = 3, District/Association/Parish = 2, and Church = 1.

1.   The conference that will best fit my budget is: _____

2.   The conference that offers me the best training potential is: _____

3.   The conference that appears to offer the best facilitators is: _____

4.   The conference that offers the best location in my view is: _____

Score:
   14-16   National
   11-13   State
    8-10   District/Association/Parish
    4-7   Church

89. Self-study (Free - Low Cost)
Recently, I received an e-mail from a pastor who attended a ministers' meeting in which I shared my previous book, *Built By*

The Owner's Design. He stated that because of family financial concerns he could not purchase the book, but would like to purchase it at a later date. Sometimes training at group conferences is cost prohibitive. Other family and church issues may keep us from attending training opportunities. If so, self-study is a viable option.

Computers have made information so accessible. In addition, the proliferation of books, manuals, and video series makes self-study an excellent alternative. Though video series are a high-cost item, many states and local church libraries have these on file.

How does one begin to put together a plan of self-study? One option is to borrow or buy an already existing book or training resource. The benefit is that the material is self-contained. All you need to do is follow the outline. The downside of this approach is that more than likely the resource will contain material that is of little or no value to you.

Another option, though more time consuming, is to tailor-make a syllabus that is geared to specific needs you have as teacher. Once you have that outline, look for specific resources that speak to those issues. This option is definitely more work but will probably have a more lasting effect on your training.

Tool Time

Self-study considerations
- Locate a place in your home or office with the least noise and interruptions.
- Choose a time daily that you will engage in study. Protect that time from interruptions. Allow for interruptions only in the case of an emergency.
- Discuss with your spouse your plans and ask for limited interruptions. Share that you will make up the lost time with family. Be sure you do.
- Commit to put into practice one new skill learned each week.

Teaching demands that we never stop learning. Once we stop, effectiveness begins to dwindle. Teachers owe it to their pupils to stay on the cutting edge. Excellence becomes impossible when it is based on knowledge we gained five, two, or one year ago. We must constantly be addressing weaknesses and upgrading our strengths. Attending group training or engaging in self-study will improve our chances of moving forward in effectiveness.

---

1. John Maxwell, *The 21 Irrefutable Laws of Leadership* (Nashville, Tennessee: Thomas Nelson Publishers, 1998), pp. 23-24.

Chapter 17

Tools That Involve Discipleship

Two gas company servicemen, a senior training supervisor and a young trainee, were out checking meters in a suburban neighborhood. They parked their truck at the end of the alley and worked their way to the other end. At the last house, a woman looking out her kitchen window watched the two men as they checked the gas meter.

Finishing the meter check, the senior supervisor challenged his younger co-worker to a foot race down the alley back to the truck to prove that an older guy could outrun a younger one.

As they came running up to the truck, they realized the lady from the last house was huffing and puffing right behind them. They stopped immediately and asked her what was wrong. Gasping for breath she replied, "When I see two gas men running as hard as you two were, I figured I'd better run, too!"[1]

Though humorous as this story is, several truths can be gained related to discipleship.

• Those we disciple will accept a challenge when asked.

- Someone is usually watching our actions.
- If we run hard concerning issues of life and death, we'll find others running hard behind us.

Dwight L. Moody had it right when he said, "It is better to train ten people than to do the work of ten people. But it is harder." The following tools are given to help us run hard in the Christian walk ... and carry others with us.

90. Prayer Partners (Free)

Pairing your class or classes into prayer partners using older members with younger members will facilitate growth in each other's prayer life. Prayer partners do several things:
- assure prayer is being given on behalf of the class and teacher,
- bring in accountability, and
- keep a spiritual focus among class members.

Allow class members to choose their partner as long as the younger/older prerequisite is maintained. Ask they get together as often as possible to pray — at least once a week. Encourage them to keep prayer journals.

Within class meetings, allow prayer partners to get together for a brief time before class starts or ends. Occasionally let them share answers to prayer. Keeping with the mandate for Sunday school about life change, stress the need of prayer partners to pray for the lost.

Prayer partnering helps fight spiritual battles. "In an age in which the stakes are growing ever higher in the daily spiritual battles of all people, prayer is indisputably one of the greatest and most underutilized weapons we have at our disposal."[2] Sunday school classes that make prayer a priority, grow.

91. Discipleship Partners (Free)

A step beyond prayer partners is discipleship partners. These may not be the same people who are prayer partners, though they most naturally can be. These accountability partners are also paired on the basis of young with mature Christian.

108

Discipleship partners engage each other in areas of solitude, seeking, service, sacrifice, and soul winning: solitude by having a personal quite time; seeking by pursuing godliness; service by working for Christ's kingdom where they live; sacrifice by dying daily to self; and soul winning by witnessing to our lost world. "Bible teaching, including Sunday school and other forms of discipleship, to be effective, must be done in the context of evangelism."[3] Prayer and Bible study are a part of such times together.

Tool Resource
Discipleship partner accountability form

1. Solitude — I had my quiet time daily this week.
    yes _____ no _____

2. Seeking — I can honestly say I pursued godliness this week.
    yes _____ no _____

3. Service — I worked for Christ this week through his church.
    yes _____ no _____

4. Sacrifice — I died daily to self this week.
    yes _____ no _____

5. Soul Winning — I actively shared my faith this week with someone who was lost.
    yes _____ no _____

Discipleship is an ongoing process that will never be complete until we go home to be with our Lord. Until then, we are constantly in a state of helping ourselves and each other become more and more like Jesus. Prayer and discipleship partners are two tools that can bring spiritual maturity closer to reality.

---

1. The Sermon Illustrator. Internet online. Available from <www.net153.com/illustrations/discipleship.shtml>.

2. George Barna, "Successful Churches: What They Have In Common," Barna Research Group, 1990, p. 15.

3. John Slack, Lessons From Church Growth Research. Internet online. Available from <home.snu.edu~hculbert.fs/Learn.htm>.

Chapter 18

Tools That Use Planning

John Maxwell tells the story of two explorers: Norwegian explorer Roald Amundsen and a British navel officer, Robert Falcon Scott. Both took teams to the south pole. One team triumphantly made the journey unscathed. The other perished in their attempt. Maxwell says, "Because Robert Falcon Scott was unable to live by the law of navigation, he and his companions died by it."[1] The law of navigation involves detail planning.

Sunday schools across our land are struggling or dying because we have not planned our navigation charts to address lack of purpose, goal absence, faulty action plans, and little or no follow-up.

92. Mission Statement (Free)

"Jesus knew his mission statement, and he did not deviate from it."[2] The average Sunday school member is clueless as to his/her church mission statement ... if the church has one.

In research done for *Built By The Owner's Design: The Positive Approach To Building Your Church God's Way*, 51 percent of

Southern Baptist, 100 percent of United Methodist, and 66 percent of Presbyterian USA churches said their church had adopted a church mission statement in a business session.

In the 2003 BSSQ survey churches, 86 percent said their church had a church mission statement. Having such a statement is encouraging ... and is a first step.

Considering the massive decline in several of these mainline denominations, one would think a mission statement does not have much influence on growth. On the contrary, these figures contradict that statement until you see that 65 percent of the SBC, 60 percent of UMC, and 77 percent of the PUSA churches had no long-range plan. Though 100 percent of the Presbyterian USA Churches I surveyed said they had a mission statement, 77 percent had no plans in place to fulfill their mission.

My recent 2003 BSSQ survey supports that original research in that while 86 percent had a mission statement, 52 percent had no goals to fulfill the statement or action plans to reach their goals. A mission statement alone will not impact growth, but coupled with the setting of goals and action plans to meet goals, it has everything to do with growth.

When writing your mission statement, consider the following:

- Don't write it alone. Unless the church family feels it belongs to them, they won't support it.
- Base whatever statement you come up with on the Great Commission. This is the church's marching orders. Any statement must include reaching a lost world for Christ.
- Set up a mission statement ministry team that includes a cross section of the congregation.
- Go slow. Be thorough.
- Make the statement short, catchy, and easy to memorize.
- Design a promotion plan to make the statement memorable to the congregation. Make sure every piece of correspondence, bulletin, newsletter, and memo has the printed statement.
- Implement creative ways the congregation can say, see, and hear the statement in worship services.
- You've succeeded if the average member can recall the statement when asked.

93. Goal Setting (Free)

In the long run, men only hit what they aim at.
— Henry David Thoreau

"Former Senator Dwight W. Morrow searched in vain to find his railroad ticket as he was on a train leaving New York City. 'I must find that ticket,' he muttered. The conductor, who stood waiting beside him, said, 'Don't worry about it, Mr. Morrow. We know you had a ticket. Just mail it to the railroad when you find it.' 'That's not what's troubling me,' replied Morrow. 'I need to find it to know where I'm going.' "[3]

Goals are our tickets to tell us where we're going. They are written to support and complete the mission statement.

Remember to go to God first. Hudson Taylor had definite convictions about how God's work should be done. We can make our best plans and try to carry them out in our own strength, or we can make careful plans and ask God to bless them. Yet another way is to begin working with God, to ask his plans, and to offer ourselves to carry out his purposes.[4] Ultimately his purposes are all that really matter.

When writing goals, make them measurable and specific. Also make them attainable, but not with human effort. Goals for the Sunday school must have a godlike quality to them. Rick Warren, pastor of the great Saddleback Church likes adding a zero to his goals. For instance, if he has 10,000 prospects, he sets a goal of 100,000 prospects.

Your class or the classes you manage may not be able to go from thirty members to 300, but they surely can go to 150. Such a number is godlike. If you are in a rural area or populace that is declining, such goals may seem beyond impossible. Yet, very few communities have more than 50 percent of their population in church on a given Sunday.

Do a brief assessment and then set basic Sunday school class goals. If you are a church leader, complete this process for every class.

Where we are: As of _____ (date)
- our class enrollment was _____.
- our number of prospects on file _____.
- our average attendance was _____.

Believing that it is the Lord's will that we grow, we commit to increase
- our Sunday school class enrollment to _____, by _____ (date).
- our number of prospects in this file to _____, by _____ (date).
- our average attendance to _____, by _____ (date).

As pastor or education minister, you will also want to set a goal for the number of class units (classes).

94. Action Plans (Free)

Plan ahead. It was not raining when Noah built the ark. — Source unknown

Specific steps are set in motion with action plans to reach goals. Make them time sequential. One step at a time moves you closer to reaching the goal. If your actions are to include an event, be sure to write out a promotional calendar. Many Sunday school activities and events fail because of poor promotion.

Use the following chart to write out your strategy plans:

Projects and actions	People assigned to	Dates	Resources/ funds needed
_____	_____	_____	_____
_____	_____	_____	_____
_____	_____	_____	_____
_____	_____	_____	_____

Tool Resource

Annual planner

The theme of the Sunday School Annual Planner and CD changes each year, but it is available at all Lifeway Christian bookstores, or from <www.lifeway.com>.

95. Follow-up/Evaluation (Free)

Sunday school class planning needs follow-up. If prospects were revealed, were they visited? If physical needs were present, were action plans carried out successfully to meet the needs? If names surfaced needing a salvation presentation, was the delivery given?

The following questions can help in determining our success in reaching goals and fulfilling our mission statement. Go through the questions for each goal that was set.

1. Did we reach our goal? Why or why not?

2. Did we complete each action? Why or why not?

3. Did the goal successfully help fulfill our mission statement?

4. What could we have done differently to better reach the goal?

5. What was lacking in the form of resources?

6. What is the class leadership reaction to our reaching or not reaching this goal?

7. Does this goal need immediate follow-up to maximize its benefit? If so, what needs to be done?

8. How was God seen in fulfilling this goal?

Evaluation and follow-up are helpful in learning about what didn't work. They also can encourage Sunday school leadership by soaking in all that was accomplished. In addition, evaluation raises the success curve for the coming year as lessons learned are applied to the new year's planning.

---

1. John Maxwell, *The Irrefutable Laws of Leadership* (Nashville, Tennessee: Thomas Nelson Publishers, 1998), p. 36.

2. Laurie Beth Jones, *Jesus, CEO* (New York: Hyperion, 1995), p. 13.

3. *Daily Bread*, September 11, 1992. Internet online. Available from <www.sermonillustrations.com/a-z/d/destination.htm>.

4. Warren Wiersbe, *Handbook of Preaching and Preachers* (Chicago, Illinois: Moody Publishers, 1984), p. 243.

Chapter 19

Teacher Enlistment Tools

Pity the minister of education. The selection process started late stacked with senior adults whose primary interest was their age group. They proceeded to enlist new teachers without job descriptions, asking for commitment to service in the hallways.

Infinite variations exist of the testimony of one committee member: "Let's get this over with. Most of our teachers will come back next year. We have our senior classes, so a quick call is all we need for the other classes."

The minister of education stares down at the finished product. The report on teacher enlistment is going to the church for approval. He knows it will be approved. He knows it will be another less than fruitful year in Sunday school work.

And on it goes, through one church year after another with poorly enlisted teachers, wrongly placed emphasis, and ultimately, inadequate religious education. But the minister of education keeps working, hoping for leaders who see the potential consequences of their decisions — those willing to grapple with what's best for the entire church body.

Through the years, I have witnessed numerous selection teams at work — most stumbling through the process of teacher enlistment. The reasons for those failures are surprisingly few. I see the same mistakes over and over. After comparing notes with leaders in the field, I've narrowed the list to just four. Call them the deadliest pitfalls of teacher enlistment.

96. Timing (Free)

Enlistment involves the appropriate amount and use of time. The smaller the church, the smaller the amount of time needed. Praying over, assigning of contacts, and the actual enlistment takes adequate time to accomplish the task.

The Pitfall: The selection process is prone to begin work late. Sometimes, it is not their fault. If the leadership in charge is late submitting or securing a selection team, its starting date is pushed back — delaying the work.

The Solution: Place the expected starting date for the selection team in your policies and procedures manual. This date should be in April at the latest, especially if your church year is starting in September to coincide with literature changes. If this is not possible, have it understood with your pastor, staff, and church council when the selection team work should begin. To delay the electing and starting of the committee's work is to reap a rushed enlistment — causing the potential for headaches in coming months.

97. Selection Team (Free)

The selection team should be made up of a broad cross section of your congregation — evenly divided between men and women, young and old alike. It should include members who know the congregation, yet not exclude someone just because they do not. A committee made up of active church members is usually the norm.

The Pitfall: Churches tend to swing the pendulum too far in either direction. Either they include too many of one gender who know the congregation or they get the sexes equal but include a number who are unfamiliar with the congregation. It is a fact that men and women do think differently — even in the matter of teacher enlistment. The real danger comes when a member enlists those unqualified who lack prior knowledge of the congregation.

Another serious pitfall is the enlisting of church family who are unfaithful in their attendance. Chances are, if they don't attend Sunday school regularly, they are not going to serve faithfully as a teacher.

The Solution: Keep tabs on the ratio of men to women, young to old. Ask questions about each nominee. Do they attend faithfully? How well do they know the membership? Do the nominees have a genuine concern for the church and its education work?

98. Procedure For Enlistment (Free)

Several surveys of clergy, including a study of over 1,000 pastors, revealed the number one church problem is finding enough people to accomplish the educational program.[1] The reason so many churches come up short in finding people to serve is they fall for some obvious traps.

The Pitfall: Many teachers feel no one cares because of the impersonal way they were recruited. Others feel they were abandoned by the church when they served the same class for multiple years without a word of thanks, appreciation, or encouragement. Many quit and we are left wondering what happened. What now? Still others become discouraged when the decisions they make as a teacher are overruled by the deacon body before the church gets a chance to weigh those decisions.

The Solution: Avoid impersonal pleas made in the bulletin, newsletter, and pulpit. Personal contacts are essential — with one-on-one encounters in the home being the best. Give potential members a job description, defining the position and the relationships. It should also include precise statements regarding the responsibilities of the teacher. The job description should also include a service contract — usually a one year appointment.

To avoid teachers feeling deserted and no one caring, regular ways of affirming teachers should be put in place. Fall teacher banquets, high attendance days, and special days in their personal lives (such as birthdays or anniversaries) are ideal ways to let teachers know they are appreciated.

99. Prayer In Selection (Free)

Our source of power comes in the form of prayer. We go to our heavenly Father for guidance and confirmation — guidance, in seeking the right people to serve, confirmation, in their accepting God's call. The end result is the right teacher teaching the right class.

The Pitfall: The danger comes in three ways: one, when we fail to pray; two, when prayer becomes ritualistic; three, when we pray generally. To fail to pray is to lose God's way and accomplish only what man can do. To pray ritualistically is to have a form of godliness but deny the power thereof. Its part in enlistment is no better than not praying. To pray generally is to admit our insincerity — lacking the spiritual fortitude necessary to meet specific enlistment needs.

The Solution: Pray before, during, and after every enlistment team meeting. Pray earnestly. Seek God's face. Allow a week before your next meeting to pray over the church roster.

Remove any hint of ritualistic praying by constantly asking throughout enlistment meetings, "Who does God want us to ask to serve?" If no answer comes, keep praying until it does.

Be specific in your praying. Ask God for members by name. Once individuals have been chosen to approach, pray for God's conviction concerning their willingness to serve. Be precise about everything in the enlistment process when you approach God in prayer.

The benefits of avoiding these enlistment perils are worth making the effort to implement their solutions.

The following summarizes how our skirting these pitfalls will make enlistment a joy.

• Early enlistment of your enlistment team will provide more time for discussion and prayer.
• A diverse team makeup will address every teacher selection with integrity.
• A consensus will be reached on priority enlistment needs after a week of prayer.
• Home visits with job descriptions in hand will leave you feeling confident that this will be your best year ever.

- Saturating everything with prayer will open doors and hearts to people who previously were not involved.

Recently, I read of a team of novice mountain climbers who lost their lives ascending Mount Everest. They had failed to consider the perils of the climb. We may not lose lives from teacher enlistment, but definitely, potential life will be sapped from our church when we ignore the pitfalls. Avoiding them will insure that timing, selection team makeup, teaching procedures, and prayer are implemented at their optimum levels.

---

1. James A. Sheffield and Tim J. Holcomb, *Church Officer And Committee Guidebook, Revised* (Nashville, Tennessee: ConventionPress, 1992), p. 18.

Chapter 20

A Tool Of Understanding

The fall attendance campaign melted our resolve. Hoping beyond hope, we had envisioned a more productive emphasis. Reality seared its message of disappointment — deeply rooting it in our souls. We had prayed. We had visited. We had called. Few had come. Our utter amazement caused one perceptive layman to ask, "Could it be that lost people know something we don't?"

His question prompted my curiosity. Yes indeed, they know some things we don't. Things that must grab hold of our spirits if we are to do outreach that pays off for Sunday school and Christ's kingdom.

100. Knowing The Lost (Free)
1. A Lost Person Knows: "I can be reached if you don't give up."

Experts tell us it takes thirteen contacts before a person will respond to our invitation to come to Sunday school and church. We often quit after one or two unproductive encounters. Surely if a soul is worth saving, it's worth unceasing expressions of concern and interest.

Recently, an elderly Sunday school teacher told me, "Brother Danny, I have a lady on my roll that I have invited for years and years to Sunday school to no avail. Guess what? Sunday she was in my class." I rejoiced with her because she understood the principle of "loving without ceasing." Some people take longer to accept our invitations. Many are just wanting to see how genuinely interested we are in them. They know we must truly love them when we keep coming back after repeated rejections.

I asked our 2003 BSSQ survey churches this question: "How does your church rate in 'seeing the multitudes, and having compassion'?" On a scale of one to ten, with ten being the highest, a response of six or above was shown by 76 of the responders. Only 15 percent responded with a five or below — no one under four.

When making continual contacts, please consider these issues:
- Frequent contacts should not be pushy and obnoxious. If you sense in any way a resentful spirit, back off. Wait a few weeks. Ask someone else to make the next contact or go yourself.
- Keep visits short.
- Avoid meal times.
- Vary your means of contact. Use cards, letters, telephone calls, and personal visits alternately.
- Meet a need or help in times of crisis. When doing so, avoid giving your invitation at that time.

2. A Lost Person Knows: "I will come and stay as long as I sense you care."

Most of us in Sunday school say we think lost people will come if we just show them we care. We declare we know this, yet our actions say otherwise. What we really think, we really do.

Consider these uncaring comments:
- "Ma'am, you're in my seat."
- "You're not from around here are you?"
- "My kids may have to go to school with them but they don't have to be at Sunday school."

Our uncaring at times is very subtle. Consider these:

- A sign on the outside basketball court that reads in bold red letters, "For church members only."
- Announcement in the worship service: "Come join our basketball team today at 4 p.m. To join, you must be a church member."
- A visit to a home to ask people to Sunday school, yet missing their family crisis two weeks earlier.

We can show we really care by:

- Avoiding exclusive language in our conversations and activities.
- Meeting needs in times of crisis.
- Using kind words of love, concern, interest, and encouragement.
- Praying for them in their homes about issues of importance.

3. A Lost Person Knows: "I don't resent you sharing your faith."

Nine out of ten pastors call their church evangelistic. However, less than one out of three church attendees has shared his/her faith with a non-Christian within the past twelve months. Though other reasons can be given for some of this timidity, it is clear many do not venture a verbal witness because of fear ... fear of rejection ... fear of resentment.

After 25 years of ministry and hundreds of witnessing opportunities, only one person has ever resented me sharing my faith. The vast majority have politely listened to my testimony. Some have come to know Christ as their personal Lord and Savior. Practically all, with the one exception, have appreciated my concern. The lone objector, I believe, will one day thank me in heaven for planting a seed.

When sharing your faith, consider the following:

- Cold call evangelism is still effective. When relationship building is not possible because of time restraints, give a witness. If you know you will only see the person once in your life, don't let it be a missed opportunity.
- Live your faith. A verbal witness is no good without a life that backs it up. Conversely, a godly life is not enough for a lost person to come to Christ. We must verbally tell them how.

- A verbal outburst of, "You're going to hell if you don't repent," is counterproductive. Such discharge will bring resentment like none other ... and rightly so. The reality of hell can be shared without verbal abuse.

4. A Lost Person Knows: "I see through attempts to reach me when I'm treated as a number."

One must distinguish between counting people and people counting numbers. We count people so as to measure how effective we are doing in reaching others. People counting numbers, on the other hand, is cold-handedly counting bodies with little interest in their wants, needs, and spiritual condition. Masquerading such outreach attempts is ultimately futile. The lost read right through it.

After a successful Sunday school campaign, First Church was proud of the numbers reached. The Sunday following proved how false their attempts of care and concern. Jeannie, the track coach and a recent new church member, brought a friend. During the time of welcome, no one greeted Jeannie and her friend. The next week the staff learned that neither Jeannie nor her companion would ever be back. Jeannie said, "I and my guest were just a number. To the church we were a body to be counted, not persons to be loved and nurtured."

We can avoid such allegations by doing the following:
- Address all the biblical passages related to numbers before presenting any effort to increase attendance.
- Stress in all correspondence, printed promotional material, and verbal announcements attempts in reaching people.
- Meet needs first. Invite second.

5. A Lost Person Knows: "I respect and respond to a godly life."

My father-in-law openly shares his faith. Being the treasurer of his local welders union for 25 years kept him at odds with union leaders less than honest with their money management. Butting heads was common. Yet, now eighty years old, Doc has had many an opportunity to lead some of these men to the Lord while on their death beds. Why? They respected Doc Allen. They remembered his testimony. He lived what he said he believed. Now dying, they wanted the same Jesus that Doc knew.

We have chosen to believe lost people want little to do with us and our faith. No, they just want to see something genuine. Though rejection may linger and disrespectful comments may be made, lost people eventually come around. Down deep they respect our stand. Many wish they had such resolve. Our task is to live a loving and godly life before them.

To gain such respect, consider the following:

- Godliness on Sunday with worldly actions through the week is a turn-off. Confess, repent, and begin to live a consistent godly life. Educate Sunday school members in the matter.
- Take steps to improve spirituality. Major on discipleship. Move the Sunday school family to the next level.
- Stay in touch with the lost during times of crisis. More than likely, if they are going to turn to Christ, it will be then. A crisis triggers seeing Christ in you. Your presence and their respect opens the potential for a verbal witness.

What the lost know and we don't know can mean their being lost for an eternity. It's time we educate ourselves and use the tool of knowing the lost. Never giving up, truly caring, sharing our faith, avoiding the numbers game, and gaining respect are simple, but profound keys to opening the floodgates of the lost to our church. Such knowledge frees us to impact our world. May we never again be in the dark concerning what the lost know so that our Sunday schools may bring them to the light.

These 100 tools for building Sunday school by the Owner's Design are only effective if put to use. As you do many simultaneously, you will see small spurts of growth. Once they mesh into the mainstream of Sunday school life, ripples of excitement, energy, and engagement will become obvious. In due time, the overflow gates will open to growth ... and you will relish each and every tool that God used to bring it about.

Appendix I

Building Sunday School/Small Groups
Questionnaire Results

1. In developing the spiritual disciplines of prayer and personal Bible study, my church is:

very successful	14 percent
somewhat successful	52 percent
adequate	24 percent
poor	10 percent

2. My church people engage in the spiritual disciplines of fasting and journaling:

all the time	5 percent
most of the time	10 percent
some of the time	52 percent
never	29 percent

3. My congregation is engaged in a church-wide visitation program:

weekly	24 percent
monthly	19 percent
does not have one	43 percent
quarterly	5 percent
irregularly	5 percent

4. Our church uses the following media in promoting our church and ministries: (Please check all that apply)

_____ radio spots	14 percent
_____ television spots	24 percent

_____	newspaper articles	38 percent
_____	newspaper ads	52 percent
_____	billboards	14 percent
_____	magazine ads	5 percent
_____	community service announcements (radio, television, newspaper)	24 percent
_____	Other	
	word of mouth	24 percent
	Internet	5 percent
	flier distribution	10 percent
	None	5 percent

5. My church considers enrolling people in Sunday school/small groups:

extremely important	43 percent
important	38 percent
somewhat important	14 percent
not important	0 percent

6. The effectiveness of my church in enrolling people in Sunday school/small groups is:

excellent	14 percent
good	24 percent
fair	33 percent
poor	14 percent

7. My church has (please check all that apply):

_____	greeters	86 percent
_____	welcome center	43 percent

8. My church makes every attempt to enlist Sunday school/small group teachers who have the spiritual gift of teaching:

always	33 percent
most of the time	52 percent
sometimes	10 percent
never	5 percent

9. My church views the way we keep our facilities as:

very important	43 percent
important	48 percent
somewhat important	5 percent
of no importance	0 percent

10. My church engages in Sunday school campaigns and high attendance days: (all that apply)

4 times a year	_____	10 percent
3 times a year	_____	33 percent
2 times a year	_____	12 percent
1 time a year	_____	30 percent
never	_____	10 percent
other every Sunday		5 percent

11. We, as a church, network with our local, state, and national offices for help in training and resources:

often	19 percent
sometimes	48 percent
seldom	10 percent
never	14 percent
not applicable	5 percent

12. We have a system in place for discovering prospects:

yes	71 percent
no	29 percent

13. We offer training for our teachers:

yearly	43 percent
quarterly	18 percent
monthly	15 percent
weekly	10 percent
never	14 percent

14. Our church has: (Check all that apply)

a mission statement _____	86 percent
set goals to fulfill statement _____	48 percent
action plans to reach goals _____	48 percent

15. How does your church rate in "seeing the multitudes, and having compassion"? (On a scale of 1-10 with 10 being the highest)

1	0 percent
2	0 percent
3	0 percent
4	5 percent
5	10 percent
6	19 percent
7	14 percent
8	14 percent
9	24 percent
10	10 percent

Appendix II

The Building Sunday School
By The Owner's Design Tools
In Order Of Importance

This list can only be an approximation. The importance of these tools will depend on the church leader (pastor, staff, Sunday school teacher), denomination affiliation, and church.

The author welcomes your suggestions for changing these for future updates. He encourages you to rearrange your list based on your experiences so that it makes sense to you. Then send it back to him. He appreciates your help. Send to: Danny Von Kanel, 826 10th Avenue, Franklinton, LA 70438.

Thank you!

Tools

1. God — Our Most Powerful Resource
2. You
3. Pastor
4. Staff
5. Deacons
6. Sunday School/Small Group Leaders
7. Congregation
8. Personal Quiet Time
9. Personal Bible Study
10. Prayer
11. Worship
12. Prayer Partners
13. Discipleship Partners
14. Love
15. Mission Statement
16. Goal Setting
17. Action Plans
18. Follow-up/Evaluation
19. FAITH
20. GROW — Outreach Teams That Win
21. Weekly Visitation
22. Forty Men And Forty Women For God On Visitation
23. Space
24. Community Awareness Evangelism
25. Knowing The Lost
26. Comprehension Evangelism
27. Confirmation Evangelism
28. Conversion Evangelism
29. Home Bible Study
30. High Attendance Days
31. Fasting
32. Creature Comforts
33. Word Of Mouth
34. Consistency

35. Accountability
36. Simplicity
37. Creativity
38. Professionalism
39. Optimism
40. Courage
41. Enthusiasm
42. Excellence
43. Clean Facilities
44. Variety
45. Group Training
46. Self-study
47. Four-week Emphasis
48. Thirteen-week Emphasis
49. Telephone Calls/Letters/ Postcards
50. Stacking
51. Commitment Seekers
52. Enrollment Visitation
53. Visitor Enrollment
54. Enrollment Goals
55. Cold Call Enrollment
56. Event Enrollment
57. Timing
58. Selection Team
59. Procedure For Enlistment
60. Prayer In Selection
61. Spiritual Gift Of Teaching
62. Love Of Age Group
63. Leadership
64. Flexibility
65. Knowledge
66. Support
67. Door-to-Door Canvassing
68. Telephone Survey
69. New Connects
70. School Annuals
71. State Sunday School Leaders
72. Director Of Missions, District Director, Or Parish Minister
73. Associational, District, Or Parish Sunday School Directors
75. Marriage Enrichment Weekends
76. Literacy Classes
77. Sports Teams
78. Weekday Early Education
79. Mother's Day Out
80. Newspaper
81. Radio
82. Television
83. Newsletter
84. Bulletin
85. Website
86. E-mail
87. Greeters
88. Welcome Center
89. Outreach Leaders
90. Records
91. Thank-you Notes
92. News Releases
93. Speed
94. Journaling
95. Directional Signs
96. Agility
97. Room Preparation
98. Stationery
99. Business Cards
100. School/Civic Program Ad

www.ingramcontent.com/pod-product-compliance
Lightning Source LLC
LaVergne TN
LVHW021510080426
835509LV00018B/2473